the PARTRIDGE and the PEAR

A Collection of Recipes for

The Twelve Days of Christmas

Downey, Jensen & Rognehaugh

the Partridge and the Pear

A Collection of Recipes for The Twelve Days of Christmas

Published by Free Esprits

6991 South Poplar Way
Centennial City, CO 80112
FreeEsprit.com

Cover Art: Donna Downey
Photography: Jacqulin Rognehaugh
Introductions: Lisa Jensen

This cookbook is a collection of favorite recipes,
which are not necessarily original recipes.

ISBN-10: 0-9786878-0-9
ISBN-13: 978-0-9786878-0-9

Edited, Designed, and Manufactured by
Favorite Recipes® Press
an imprint of

FRP

P.O. Box 305142
Nashville, Tennessee 37230
800-358-0560

Manufactured in China
First Printing: 2007
3,000 copies

Dedication

This cookbook is a celebration of the birth of Christ.

It is dedicated to Don and Geneva Wilson,
our inspiration for the adventure.

Lisa Jensen's recipes are dedicated to
her father Kenneth Jensen.

Special thanks to

Doris Fuller, our favorite elf.

My close friends at Sandhill, especially to Lisa Stewart and Jean Osborn for their willingness to sample our menus and Jean for allowing us to share her Fresh Tomato Bisque and homemade ice cream recipes.

Thank you to Matt and Tom Downey their suggestions on the recommended wines and their thoughtful opinions.

The Csordas Family, for first sharing this tradition with us.

Richard, for his support throughout this adventure.

Foreword

Almost every passionate pursuit has an interesting story, and we think you'll enjoy the story of how the idea for *The Partridge and the Pear* began. Over a period of five years, five siblings had an idea to secretly send a gift to their parents on each of the Twelve Days of Christmas. Through creative discussions that brought the family closer together, each of the gifts were selected in terms of something that was not only appropriate within the original "Twelve Days" tradition, but was also fun to experience. Many of the gifts included the elements of superb cuisine.

So, each of the gifts were quietly delivered at midnight to otherwise unsuspecting parents in a quiet town. By the third night, the Secret Santa noticed that the houselights came on within minutes of the clock striking twelve, in anticipation of the next day's gift.

In the following years, the gifts were newly created. Over time, the planning discussion brought the family together in energetic and often wild discussions of what might make the perfect "5 Golden Rings" or "2 Turtle Doves" for the coming year's ensemble. As momentum and anticipation built year after year, what originally was a September through October planning season began as early as the following spring.

Among the most untraditional gifts, was a noncaloric idea for "4 Calling Birds"—the outcome was a quartet of holiday carolers singing on the front porch to the bewildered recipients who were asking, "Who sent you?"

It is our hope that with *The Partridge and the Pear* you might save a little of the time required for planning superb holiday menus, and we also hope that it will bring you closer together with your children, grandchildren, friends, neighbors, or business associates. And with the same mystery that we celebrate our favorite holiday, we trust that you will anticipate each day within this season, as well as enjoy our ideas for years to come.

Bon appétit!
Richard Rognehaugh

On the first day of Christmas,
my true love sent to me:
A partridge in a pear tree.

On the second day of Christmas,
my true love sent to me:
Two turtle doves,
And a partridge in a pear tree.

On the third day of Christmas,
my true love sent to me:
Three French hens,
Two turtle doves,
And a partridge in a pear tree.

On the fourth day of Christmas,
my true love sent to me:
Four calling birds,
Three French hens,
Two turtle doves,
And a partridge in a pear tree.

On the fifth day of Christmas,
my true love sent to me:
Five golden rings,
Four calling birds,
Three French hens,
Two turtle doves,
And a partridge in a pear tree.

On the sixth day of Christmas,
my true love sent to me:
Six geese a-laying,
Five golden rings,
Four calling birds,
Three French hens,
Two turtle doves,
And a partridge in a pear tree.

On the seventh day of Christmas,
my true love sent to me:
Seven swans a-swimming,
Six geese a-laying,
Five golden rings,
Four calling birds,
Three French hens,
Two turtle doves,
And a partridge in a pear tree.

On the eighth day of Christmas,
my true love sent to me:
Eight maids a-milking,
Seven swans a-swimming,
Six geese a-laying,
Five golden rings,
Four calling birds,
Three French hens,
Two turtle doves,
And a partridge in a pear tree.

On the ninth day of Christmas,
my true love sent to me:
Nine ladies dancing,
Eight maids a-milking,
Seven swans a-swimming,
Six geese a-laying,
Five golden rings,
Four calling birds,
Three French hens,
Two turtle doves,
And a partridge in a pear tree.

On the tenth day of Christmas,
my true love sent to me:
Ten lords a-leaping,
Nine ladies dancing,
Eight maids a-milking,
Seven swans a-swimming,
Six geese a-laying,
Five golden rings,
Four calling birds,
Three French hens,
Two turtle doves,
And a partridge in a pear tree.

On the eleventh day of Christmas,
my true love sent to me:
Eleven pipers piping,
Ten lords a-leaping,
Nine ladies dancing,
Eight maids a-milking,
Seven swans a-swimming,
Six geese a-laying,
Five golden rings,
Four calling birds,
Three French hens,
Two turtle doves,
And a partridge in a pear tree.

On the twelfth day of Christmas,
my true love sent to me:
Twelve drummers drumming,
Eleven pipers piping,
Ten lords a-leaping,
Nine ladies dancing,
Eight maids a-milking,
Seven swans a-swimming,
Six geese a-laying,
Five golden rings,
Four calling birds,
Three French hens,
Two turtle doves,

And a partridge in a pear tree!

Table of Contents

Welcome to The Partridge and the Pear *cookbook! We hope you find our information, recipes, menus, and resources to be both fun and informative. If you enjoy cooking over the holidays, but have a difficult time coming up with new and exciting menus, this cookbook should assist you in fixing your holiday hunger with something out of the ordinary.*

Traditionally, the Twelve Days of Christmas are celebrated starting on the 26th of December through the 6th of January, which is the day of Epiphany on the Christian calendar. We have heard of people beginning December 14th and ending on the 25th. Some even start it on the 25th going through to the 5th.

No matter how you celebrate the holidays, or whether you celebrate the Twelve Days of Christmas at all, we hope our unique collection of menus will bring your family and friends closer together during your special traditions and celebrations of the season.

1 Partridge in a Pear Tree

Merry Christmas and WELCOME to the
THE FIRST DAY OF CHRISTMAS!

So, it's the first day of Christmas and just what is a partridge anyway?

Partridges are game birds that belong to the pheasant family but are much smaller than a pheasant and more resemble grouse or quail. Partridge is rarely seen on restaurant menus; however, quail and pheasant are frequently served in gourmet restaurants, especially those that carry a French theme. Though not seen on many modern menus, the famed Pheasant Under Glass was wildly popular years ago.

Native to Europe, Asia, and Africa, the partridge was introduced to North America in 1889 when brought to Virginia. The two types seen in North America are the Chukar partridge and the Gray partridge—both only 10 to 14 inches long and weighing less than 1 pound.

During hunting season, the partridge is considered a treasured catch. And your "true love" will certainly consider YOU a treasured catch as you make this modern, classy, and truly unique game dish.

A special thanks to Lisa's mother, Edith Jensen for her recipe for Wild Rice with Mushrooms and Slivered Almonds.

Menu

Pear Salad with Goat Cheese and Partridgeberry Dressing
Partridge or Quail with Port Sauce
Wild Rice with Mushrooms and Slivered Almonds
Green Beans Parmesan
Berries en Papillote

Pinot Noir or Merlot
We recommend:
Gordon Brothers Merlot Columbia Valley 2002

Today's Menu Serves Four

The partridgeberry, also known as a lingonberry, is a sister to the blueberry and cranberry. It shares the same antioxidant qualities found in them. See our Sources on pages 114–115 to find out where to get partridgeberry products and learn what it has to do with a tickle.

Pear Salad with Goat Cheese and Partridgeberry Dressing

Partridgeberry Dressing

1/4 cup olive oil
2 tablespoons partridgeberry vinegar
1/4 teaspoon salt
1/4 teaspoon pepper

Salad

1 (6-ounce) package arugala or spinach arugula mix
1/2 cup crumbled goat cheese
1/2 cup candied walnuts or pecans
2 pears

To prepare the dressing, whisk the olive oil, vinegar, salt and pepper in a small bowl until blended.

To prepare the salad and assemble, combine the arugala, goat cheese and walnuts in a large salad bowl. Add the desired amount of the dressing and toss to coat. Cut the pears into halves and then cut each half into quarters. Divide the salad evenly among four salad plates and top each with four pear wedges.

You may substitute the partridgeberry vinegar with raspberry vinegar, which can be found in most grocery stores.

Roast Partridge or Quail with Port Sauce

Port Sauce
3 tablespoons chopped shallots
1 tablespoon butter
1 cup port
1/2 teaspoon minced fresh rosemary
1 cup chicken broth
1 to 2 tablespoons butter
Salt and pepper to taste

Partridge or Quail
8 partridge or quail (*See* Sources, pages 114–115.)
Wild Rice with Mushrooms and Slivered Almonds (page 14), or 1 package wild rice mix
1/2 teaspoon dried rosemary
1/2 teaspoon salt
1/2 teaspoon pepper
1/2 cup chicken broth
8 small sprigs of fresh rosemary

To prepare the sauce, sauté the shallots in 1 tablespoon butter for 10 minutes or until caramelized. Add the port and rosemary and bring to a boil. Cook until the mixture is reduced to 1/4 cup. Add the broth and boil until the mixture is reduced by half. Swirl in 1 tablespoon butter and taste the sauce for flavor and consistency. Add the remaining 1 tablespoon butter if needed. Season with salt and pepper. (The sauce can be made ahead the same day and reheated prior to serving.)

For the partridge, remove the giblets and neck from the birds if necessary. Rinse the birds and pat dry. (You may spatchcock or partially debone the birds at this point. *See* Sources, pages 114–115 for directions. This is optional but saves your diners from having to deal with some very small bones.)

Preheat the oven to 400 degrees. Place the birds skin side up in a 9×13-inch baking dish or pan. Stuff each bird with 4 teaspoons of Wild Rice with Mushrooms and Slivered Almonds and tie the legs together with cooking string. (If you are using deboned or partially deboned birds, the rice can be placed under each bird.) Spray the birds with nonstick cooking spray and season with dried rosemary, salt and pepper. Pour the 1/2 cup broth around the birds. Roast, uncovered, for 15 minutes. Spray with cooking spray and roast for 5 to 10 minutes longer or until the birds are cooked through.

To serve, place two partridge on each dinner plate and drizzle with approximately 1 tablespoon port sauce. Garnish each serving with a sprig of fresh rosemary.

Wild Rice with Mushrooms and Slivered Almonds

8 cups water
2 chicken bouillon cubes
8 ounces Minnesota or Canadian wild rice (no long grain included)
2 cups coarsely chopped assorted mushrooms, such as shiitake, portobello and button
2 ribs celery, chopped
1 onion, chopped
1 teaspoon dried thyme
1 tablespoon butter
3/4 cup slivered almonds
1 (14-ounce) can chicken broth
1/2 teaspoon salt
1/2 teaspoon pepper

Preheat the oven to 350 degrees. Bring the water and bouillon cubes to a boil in a large saucepan. Add the rice and reduce the heat. Cover and simmer for 1 1/4 hours. Remove from the heat and drain the rice. Return the rice to the saucepan and set aside.

Sauté the mushrooms, celery, onion and thyme in the butter in a medium sauté pan over medium-high heat for 10 minutes. Add the almonds and sauté for 5 minutes. Stir the sautéed mushroom mixture into the rice. Add the broth, salt and pepper and stir to mix well. Spoon into a 9×13-inch baking dish coated with nonstick cooking spray and cover with foil. Bake for 40 minutes.

Edith Jensen

To simplify the cooking process, any prepackaged rice mix can be substituted for this recipe. We suggest using this recipe as a stuffing for Roast Partridge or Quail with Port Sauce (page 13). The recipe should be made in advance and either kept warm or reheated while the birds are roasting.

Green Beans Parmesan

1 pound green beans, trimmed and cut into pieces
1/4 teaspoon minced garlic
1/2 teaspoon salt
1/2 teaspoon dried oregano
1 tablespoon butter
1 (8-ounce) can sliced water chestnuts, drained
1/4 cup (1 ounce) shredded Parmesan cheese

Sauté the green beans, garlic, salt and oregano in the butter in a large skillet over medium-high heat for about 5 minutes. (Adding salt to the vegetables while they cook gives them a brighter color.) Add the water chestnuts and sauté for 1 minute or until the green beans are tender but still crisp. Place in a serving dish. Add the Parmesan cheese and toss lightly.

Berries en Papillote

6 cups mixed berries, such as strawberries, blueberries, blackberries and raspberries
1/2 to 1 teaspoon sugar
1 pint vanilla frozen yogurt or ice cream

Preheat the oven to 400 degrees. Cut baking parchment into four 12-inch squares. Divide the berries into four equal portions and place on each square about a quarter of the way from the bottom of the sheet so that the top of the sheet can easily fold over the berries. Sprinkle the berries with 1/8 to 1/4 teaspoon sugar per sheet. Gently cover the berries by joining the top and bottom edges of each sheet. Fold the edges together and then fold again to seal. Seal the remaining two sides by folding each edge over twice. Secure the edges with wooden picks if necessary and place on a baking sheet. Bake for 10 minutes. Remove the packets from the oven and place on individual dessert plates or in dessert bowls. Let cool for 1 minute before opening the packets. Carefully cut a crisscross opening on the top of each packet and peel back the paper edges. Let the fruit cool for 4 to 5 minutes. Place a scoop of the frozen yogurt on each. Eat the berries right out of the packet (do not eat the baking parchment), or scoop the berries out of the packet and drizzle on top of the frozen yogurt.

Two Turtle Doves

2

Turtle doves got their name due to the gentle purring sound they make which sounds like "turr. . . turr. . ." The Latin name is streptopelia turtur. These lovely birds are on Britain's "red list," meaning they are one of approximately thirty-six species that carry the highest concern for conservation.

In celebrating the SECOND DAY OF CHRISTMAS*, we have come up with numerous dishes that carry the names of either "turtle" or "dove," but that fortunately carry no ingredients of either beloved creature.*

Menu

Fresh Veggie Salsa
Guacamole
Black Turtle Bean Chili
Hearty Turtle Bread
Turr-Turr-rific Turtle Dove Candy

Shiraz
We recommend:
d'Arenberg The Footbolt Shiraz

Today's Menu Serves Six to Eight

Steve Whitney was the one who first introduced us to using red wine vinegar as a base for fresh veggie salsa. I never got his salsa recipe, but my interpretation of his salsa has been one of our favorite dishes ever since then.

Fresh Veggie Salsa

1 cup chopped bell pepper (green, red, yellow or a mixture of each)
1/2 cup sliced green onions (about 3)
1 large tomato, seeded and chopped
1 celery rib, chopped
1 tablespoon chopped cilantro
1/2 jalapeño chile, minced (optional)
1/2 cup red wine vinegar
1/2 cup salsa (mild, medium or hot, your choice)
1 teaspoon salt
Squeeze of lemon juice or lime juice

Combine the bell pepper, green onions, tomato, celery, cilantro, jalapeño chile, vinegar, salsa, salt and lemon juice in a bowl and mix well. Chill for several hours. Serve with corn chips or celery stalks.

Jacqulin Rognehaugh

Guacamole

5 very ripe avocados, pits removed
3 garlic cloves, chopped
1 tomato, finely chopped
1 tablespoon lemon juice or lime juice
2 tablespoons sour cream
1/2 teaspoon onion powder
1 teaspoon seasoned salt
4 dashes of Tabasco sauce or your favorite hot red pepper sauce

Mash the avocados with a potato masher or a fork in a bowl. Add the garlic, tomato, lemon juice, sour cream, onion powder, seasoned salt and Tabasco sauce and mix well. Serve with corn chips or celery stalks.

Lisa Jensen

Chili is best when it is cooked all day. We suggest starting this dish early in the day.

Black Turtle Bean Chili

8 ounces dried black turtle beans
(*See* Sources, pages 114–115.)
12 cups water
1 tablespoon salt
2 pounds ground pork or turkey
1 large sweet onion, coarsely chopped
2 garlic cloves, minced
1 small green bell pepper, coarsely chopped
2 ribs celery, chopped
2 (14-ounce) cans diced tomatoes
2 (15-ounce) cans tomato sauce
1 (15-ounce) can water
1 tablespoon oregano
1 tablespoon cumin
2 tablespoons chili powder
1 teaspoon garlic powder
1 teaspoon salt
1 teaspoon pepper
1 teaspoon Tabasco sauce or your favorite hot red pepper sauce (optional)
Salt and pepper to taste

Sort and rinse the beans. Soak the beans in 4 cups of the water in a large bowl for 4 to 12 hours; drain. Place the beans in a large stockpot or Dutch oven and add the remaining 8 cups water and 1 tablespoon salt. Bring to a boil and reduce the heat. Cover and simmer for 1½ hours or until the beans are tender. Remove from the heat and drain the beans in a colander. Return the beans to the stockpot and set aside.

Brown the ground pork in a medium skillet over medium-high heat for 20 minutes, stirring constantly. Spoon the ground pork into a colander to drain, leaving the brown crumbles in the skillet. Add the onion, garlic, bell pepper and celery to the skillet. Sauté for 15 minutes or until the vegetables are tender. Add the sautéed vegetables, ground pork, undrained tomatoes, tomato sauce and the can of water to the beans and mix well, adding more or less water to reach the desired consistency. Stir in the oregano, cumin, chili powder, garlic powder, 1 teaspoon salt, the pepper and Tabasco sauce. Bring to a boil and reduce the heat. Simmer for 1 to 3 hours or until the flavors blend. (Results are best when the chili cooks for about 3 hours.) Season with salt and pepper to taste. Ladle into serving bowls and serve with sour cream, chopped green onions, guacamole, shredded Cheddar cheese and crumbled corn chips. (This dish may be made up to three months ahead and frozen in an airtight freezer-safe container.)

This is a great bread to use not only with our chili, but also for hearty ham and cheese sandwiches.

Hearty Turtle Bread

1 cup chopped sweet onion
1/2 tablespoon butter
1/2 cup chopped walnuts
1 cup (4 ounces) grated Parmesan or asiago cheese
3 cups all-purpose flour
2 teaspoons baking powder
1 teaspoon salt
1 (12-ounce) bottle of light- to medium-bodied beer
2 tablespoons butter, melted

Preheat the oven to 375 degrees. Sauté the onion in 1/2 tablespoon butter in a skillet over medium-high heat for about 5 minutes. Combine the sautéed onion, walnuts, cheese, flour, baking powder and salt in a medium bowl and stir to mix well. Add the beer gradually, stirring gently until the mixture is moist. Do not overmix. Place in a 1 1/2-quart round baking dish coated with nonstick cooking spray. (The bread can also be baked in a 5×9-inch loaf pan coated with nonstick cooking spray, but we like the round turtle look that the round baking dish provides.)

Brush the top with 1 tablespoon of the melted butter. Bake for 30 minutes. Drizzle or brush with the remaining 1 tablespoon melted butter and bake for 20 minutes longer or until a wooden pick inserted in the center comes out clean. Cool and serve.

Lisa Jensen

We added feathery white coconut and toasted the pecans to give this old classic a new twist.

Turr-Turr-rific Turtle Dove Candy

48 pecan halves
12 caramel squares
1/4 cup (heaping) shredded coconut
1/2 cup (3 ounces) semisweet chocolate chips
1/2 cup (3 ounces) white chocolate chips

Preheat the oven to 300 degrees. Place one sheet of baking parchment on a baking sheet. Arrange four of the pecan halves on the prepared baking sheet with the tips pointing out in the shape of turtle feet and with the pecan halves touching each other in the center. Carefully place one square of caramel in the center of the pecan halves, trying not to disturb the arrangement. Repeat the procedure with the remaining pecan halves and caramels to make a total of twelve turtles. Bake for 8 to 10 minutes or until the caramel just begins to soften and melt around the pecan halves, watching carefully. Remove from the oven. While the caramel is still warm, top each with about 1 teaspoon coconut and press lightly into the caramel. Let stand until cool.

Place the semisweet chocolate chips and white chocolate chips in separate sealable plastic bags. Fill a small bowl a third of the way full with hot water. Place the bags of chocolate chips in the water, making sure the water does not cover the opening of the bags. Let the bags stand in the water until the chips are completely melted.

Snip one corner of the bottom of each bag, making sure the opening is not too large. Drizzle the semisweet chocolate and then the white chocolate over the turtles on the baking sheet. Chill for 1 hour. Remove the turtles with a spatula and place in a 1-quart sealable plastic bag. Seal the bag and store in the refrigerator.

Jacqulin Rognehaugh

Three French Hens

While we could not actually find a particular species of hen called a French hen, we must then assume that the song is referring to a hen that literally came from France. For this THIRD DAY OF CHRISTMAS, we have a menu item that is, however, truly American, as we feature the Rock Cornish game hen which was originally bred by crossing a Rock hen and a Cornish hen by the well-known poultry mogul, John Tyson.

Today's menu also features a very unusual mushroom called hen-of-the-woods. Any mushroom will do for the Hen-of-the-Woods Sauce, but we think you will have a lot of fun ordering and experimenting with this unusual variety. The mushroom is also called the maitake mushroom, and grows at the foot of oak trees. The Chinese and Japanese have used the maitake for medicinal purposes, such as to enhance the immune system. And some say that it aids in preventing cancer and can lower blood pressure and assist with weight loss!

We feature maitake mushrooms in two of our menu selections as we believe that the Maitake Mushroom Risotto and Hen-of-the-Woods Sauce complement each other perfectly.

Menu

Cheddar Cheese Biscuits
Rock Cornish Game Hens with Hen-of-the-Woods Sauce
Maitake Mushroom Risotto
Sautéed Asparagus with Tomatoes
Cinnamon Apple Crepes

Chardonnay
We recommend:
Villa Maria Chardonnay Marlborough Private Bin
LEDGEWOOD CREEK Chardonnay Suisun Valley 2003

Today's Menu Serves Four

Cheddar Cheese Biscuits

2 cups all-purpose flour
1 tablespoon plus 1 teaspoon baking powder
1 teaspoon salt
2 tablespoons shortening
3/4 cup milk
3/4 cup (3 ounces) shredded Cheddar cheese

Preheat the oven to 400 degrees. Sift the flour, baking powder and salt into a bowl. Cut in the shortening with a fork until crumbly. Add the milk and toss until moistened. Stir in the cheese. Knead gently on a lightly floured surface for 5 minutes. Flatten to a 1/2-inch thickness. Cut with a 2-inch biscuit cutter. Place into twelve muffin cups sprayed with nonstick cooking spray. Bake for 8 to 10 minutes or until light brown.

Lisa Jensen

Rock Cornish Game Hens

4 Rock Cornish game hens, rinsed and patted dry
1/2 small lemon, cut into quarters
1/2 small onion, cut into quarters
1 small rib celery, cut into quarters
8 garlic cloves
Olive oil
1/2 teaspoon kosher salt
1 teaspoon pepper
1/2 teaspoon each garlic powder, thyme and paprika
Hen-of-the-Woods Sauce (page 25)

Remove the giblets from the hens and discard. Place skin side up in a large roasting pan. Fold the wings back underneath each hen, or wrap a piece of cooking string around the wings and tie at the breast. Place one lemon quarter, one onion quarter, one celery quarter and two garlic cloves in each hen cavity. Spray with cooking spray and rub with a bit of olive oil. Sprinkle inside and outside with a mixture of the seasonings. Cross the legs and tie together with cooking string. (You may make ahead the same day up to this point. Cover with foil and refrigerate.) Preheat the oven to 400 degrees. Roast the hens, uncovered, for 35 minutes. Spray with cooking spray and roast for 15 to 20 minutes or until the hens are cooked through. Cut the cooking string and scoop out the stuffing and discard. Arrange on four serving plates and top with Hen-of-the-Woods Sauce.

Hen-of-the-Woods Sauce

1/2 (.88-ounce) package dried maitake mushrooms
(*See* Sources, pages 114–115.), or
2 cups chopped fresh mushrooms
1 cup hot water
1/2 cup thinly sliced Vidalia onion or sweet onion
1 teaspoon olive oil
1/2 cup white wine
1 teaspoon dried thyme
1 1/2 tablespoons cornstarch
1 (14-ounce) can chicken broth
1/2 teaspoon salt
1/2 teaspoon pepper

Reconstitute the dried mushrooms in 1 cup hot water in a medium bowl for 15 minutes. Drain the mushrooms, reserving the liquid. (There should be about 2/3 cup liquid. The reserved liquid will give the sauce a beautiful golden brown color.)

Sauté the onion in the olive oil in a medium skillet over medium-high heat for about 5 minutes. Add the wine, drained mushrooms and thyme. Boil for 2 minutes or until the liquid evaporates, stirring frequently. Remove from the heat. Whisk the cornstarch into the reserved mushroom liquid. (If you are not using dried mushrooms, whisk the cornstarch into 2/3 cup chicken broth.) Stir the broth into the mushroom mixture. Whisk in the cornstarch mixture until blended. Return the skillet to high heat. Boil for 1 minute or until thickened, stirring constantly. Season with the salt and pepper. (The sauce can be made ahead the same day and reheated prior to serving.)

Lisa Jensen

Maitake Mushroom Risotto

4 large garlic cloves
1 teaspoon olive oil
1/2 (.88) package dried maitake mushrooms (*See* Sources, pages 114–115.), or 2 cups chopped fresh mushrooms
4 1/2 cups chicken broth
1/2 cup thinly sliced green onions (about 3 green onions)
1 teaspoon dried thyme
1 tablespoon butter
1 1/2 cups risotto or arborio rice
1/2 cup white wine
2/3 cup grated manchego cheese

Preheat the oven to 350 degrees. Place the unpeeled garlic on a piece of foil and add the olive oil. Loosely close the foil and roast for 1 hour. Remove from the oven to cool. Unwrap the garlic, remove the skins and coarsely chop. Soak the dried mushrooms in enough hot water to cover in a bowl for 15 minutes or until reconstituted; drain. Bring the broth to a boil in a medium saucepan and reduce the heat to keep the broth warm but not boiling.

Sauté the reconstituted mushrooms, green onions and thyme in the butter in a medium saucepan over medium heat for 1 minute. Add the rice and sauté for 3 minutes. Add the wine and cook until the wine is evaporated. Add the warm broth in one-ladle increments, cooking until the broth is absorbed after each addition and the rice is slightly al dente, stirring frequently. (You may not need to use all of the broth.) Remove from the heat and cool for 1 to 2 minutes. Stir in the roasted garlic and cheese. Serve immediately.

Lisa Jensen

Sautéed Asparagus with Tomatoes

24 to 32 asparagus spears, trimmed
1/2 teaspoon salt
1/2 teaspoon pepper
1/2 tablespoon olive oil
1/2 tablespoon fresh lemon juice
1 1/2 cups chopped tomatoes

Sauté the asparagus, salt and pepper in the olive oil in a large skillet over medium heat for 3 minutes. Add the lemon juice and sauté for 2 minutes or to the desired doneness. Add the tomatoes and sauté for a few seconds longer. Serve immediately.

Mark Armstrong

Cinnamon Apple Crepes

Crepes
6 tablespoons butter, melted
1/4 teaspoon salt
3 cups milk
6 eggs
1 cup all-purpose flour

Cinnamon Apple Filling
1 cup water
1 tablespoon lemon juice
3 crisp baking apples, cored and peeled
2 tablespoons butter
2 tablespoons brown sugar
1/4 teaspoon ground cinnamon
1/4 cup apple juice

To prepare the crepes, whisk 3 tablespoons of the butter, the salt, milk, eggs and flour in a mixing bowl until smooth. Cover and chill for 2 hours or longer. Heat a 10-inch skillet over medium-low heat and brush with some of the remaining butter. Heat a second skillet of the same or larger size and brush with some of the remaining butter. Pour a scant 1/3 cup of the batter in the first skillet, tilting the skillet to cover the bottom. Cook for 1 to 1 1/2 minutes or until golden. Flip the crepe into the second skillet and cook the other side until golden. (It is possible to use just one skillet, but using the second skillet helps the process go faster.) Remove the crepe and place on a plate lined with waxed paper. (Let the crepe cool before layering in the waxed paper to prevent sticking.) Continue the process with the remaining batter. (This recipe makes approximately twenty-four crepes. The crepes can be made ahead of time and frozen in an airtight container for up to 2 months.)

To prepare the filling, blend the water and lemon juice in a medium bowl. Cut the apples into thin wedges and place in the lemon water. Coat all of the apples slices well; drain. Melt the butter in a skillet over medium heat. Stir in the brown sugar and cinnamon until blended. Add the apples and sauté for 5 to 7 minutes or until tender. Stir in the apple juice and remove from the heat.

To assemble, divide the filling equally among four crepes on individual dessert plates, reserving some of the filling for the topping. Fold in four sides of each crepe to form a square. Spoon the reserved filling over the crepe squares. Serve with a small scoop of ice cream, if desired.

Four Calling Birds

4

It is believed that the calling birds referred to on the
Fourth Day of Christmas, are actually blackbirds that have
a wonderfully romantic and melodic call.
The original lyrics did not mention calling birds at all, but instead
called them colly or collie birds, which means "black."

So our theme on this Fourth Day of Christmas is black,
which may seem a bit odd for a Christmas color, but just have a look
at these recipes and you'll be singing along with the blackbirds.

Menu

Black Bean Cakes with Chipotle Aïoli
Tomato Salad with Black Olives and Feta Cheese
Twice-Baked Potatoes
Black Pepper Steaks with Bourbon Sauce
Colly Bird Cookies

Fruity heavy red Australian Shiraz
We recommend:
Woop Woop 2004 Shiraz

Today's Menu Serves Six

Black Bean Cakes with Chipotle Aïoli

Chipotle Aïoli

1/2 cup mayonnaise (you may use low-fat, but do not use fat-free)
1 rib celery, minced
1 tablespoon minced red onion
1 garlic clove, minced
1 tablespoon fresh lemon juice
1 chipotle chile in adobo sauce, chopped (*See* Sources, pages 114–115.)

Black Bean Cakes

3/4 cup chopped green bell pepper
1/2 cup finely chopped onion
2 garlic cloves, minced
1 teaspoon olive oil
1 egg
1 cup bread crumbs
1/2 cup (2 ounces) grated Parmesan cheese
1 teaspoon cayenne pepper
1 tablespoon chopped cilantro
2 (14-ounce) cans black beans, drained
2 tablespoons olive oil for frying

To prepare the aïoli, whisk the mayonnaise, celery, onion, garlic, lemon juice and chipotle chile in adobo sauce in a small bowl until well mixed. Cover and chill in the refrigerator. (You may make ahead on the same day.)

To prepare the black bean cakes, sauté the bell pepper, onion and garlic in 1 teaspoon olive oil in a small skillet over medium-high heat for 4 minutes. Whisk the egg, bread crumbs, cheese, cayenne pepper and cilantro in a medium bowl until well mixed. Add the sautéed vegetables and the drained beans and mix well with a wooden spoon, mashing some of the beans against the side of the bowl. Divide the bean mixture into six equal portions and press into six circles about 4 inches in diameter. Cook three of the cakes in 1 tablespoon of the olive oil in a large skillet over medium-high heat for 4 minutes per side. Repeat with the remaining three cakes and 1 tablespoon olive oil. Serve one cake per person topped with 1 tablespoon chipotle aïoli or serve the cakes with the chipotle aïoli on the side as an appetizer.

Lisa Jensen

Tomato Salad with Black Olives and Feta Cheese

5 large tomatoes
1 cucumber, peeled
1 small red onion, thinly sliced and separated into rings
2 (3-ounce) cans sliced black olives, drained
1 cup crumbled feta cheese
5 fresh basil leaves, thinly sliced
1/3 cup olive oil
3 tablespoons white wine vinegar
1/4 teaspoon dried dill weed
1/4 teaspoon salt
1/4 teaspoon pepper

Cut each tomato into quarters. Cut each quarter into four equal pieces. Cut the cucumber into 1/2-inch slices. Cut each slice into halves. Combine the tomatoes, cucumber, onion, olives, cheese and basil in a medium bowl. Whisk the olive oil, vinegar, dill weed, salt and pepper in a small bowl. Pour the desired amount of the dressing over the salad and toss gently to mix.

Lisa Jensen

Do not refrigerate this recipe. Tomatoes should be at room temperature when added. As a side note, tomatoes should never be refrigerated. When store bought, they can normally sit on your counter for a week.

Twice-Baked Potatoes

6 baking potatoes
1/4 cup milk
1/4 cup sour cream
2 tablespoons butter
1/4 cup (1 ounce) grated Parmesan cheese
2 green onions, finely chopped

Preheat the oven to 350 degrees. Scrub the potatoes and prick with a fork. Bake for 1 hour, turning once. Using an oven mitt, gently squeeze the potatoes to check for doneness. (The potatoes should be very soft. If not, bake for 15 minutes longer or to the desired doneness.) Remove the potatoes from the oven and let stand until cool. Cut each potato into halves and scoop the pulp into a medium saucepan, reserving firm potato shells for stuffing. Set the reserved potato shells in a 9×13-inch baking dish coated with nonstick cooking spray.

Combine the milk, sour cream and butter with the potato pulp and mash with a potato masher or electric mixer until smooth. Stir in the cheese and green onions. Fill each potato shell with equal amounts of the potato mixture. Bake for 20 minutes.

Lisa Jensen

Black Pepper Steaks with Bourbon Sauce

1/4 cup chopped shallots
2 garlic cloves, minced
1/2 tablespoon butter
1 cup shiitake mushrooms
1/2 cup bourbon
3/4 cup beef broth
1 tablespoon olive oil
6 (8-ounce) New York steaks or rib-eye steaks
3 tablespoons coarsely ground black peppercorns (McCormick's Seasoned Pepper Blend was used for testing.)
1 1/2 tablespoons kosher salt
1 tablespoon olive oil
1/4 cup cream or half-and-half

Sauté the shallots and garlic in the butter in a small skillet over medium-high heat for 3 minutes or until soft. Add the mushrooms and sauté for 2 minutes. Add the bourbon and bring to a boil. Remove from the heat and ignite with a match or utility lighter. Let the mixture burn for 30 seconds. Cover with a lid to extinguish the flame. Add the broth and boil for 3 to 4 minutes or until the mixture is reduced by half. Remove from the heat and set aside. (Getting dishes to flambé can be tricky. If you allow the bourbon to boil too long, the alcohol will burn off and the bourbon will not ignite. If you ignite the alcohol too soon and don't remove it from the heat, you can experience much bigger flames than anticipated! If you don't feel comfortable with the flambé process, the dish tastes just as good to add the bourbon and broth together and simply boil for 3 to 4 minutes.)

Using your hands, rub 1 tablespoon olive oil onto each of six steaks. Rub about 1/4 tablespoon ground peppercorns on each side of the steaks. Sprinkle kosher salt evenly on each side of the steaks. (We suggest using an outside grill to prepare the steaks to the desired degree of doneness, however, here is a pan-fried version.) Swirl the remaining 1 tablespoon of olive oil in a large heavy skillet over medium-high heat. Heat for 30 seconds or so. Add the steaks two or three at a time and cook for 3 minutes per side for medium-rare, or to the desired degree of doneness.

Reheat the bourbon sauce. Stir in the cream and cook until heated through; do not boil. (The sauce can be reheated in the skillet the steaks were fried in for added flavor.) Place the steaks on individual serving plates. Pour the sauce over the steaks, dividing evenly among the plates.

Lisa Jensen

Colly Bird Cookies

Cookies

2 1/2 cups all-purpose flour
3/4 cup sugar
1 cup (2 sticks) butter, softened
3 tablespoons cherry liqueur or cherry juice
1 teaspoon baking powder
2 teaspoons almond extract

Chocolate Cherry Glaze

4 1/2 ounces 70 percent cacao
(bittersweet) pure dark chocolate
1 tablespoon butter
1 tablespoon light corn syrup
1 to 2 tablespoons cherry liqueur or cherry juice

To prepare the cookies, combine the flour, sugar, butter, cherry liqueur, baking powder and almond extract in a mixing bowl. Beat at low speed for 2 to 3 minutes or until well mixed, scraping the bowl frequently. Divide the dough into two equal portions. Wrap each portion in plastic wrap and chill in the freezer for 1 hour or longer.

Preheat the oven to 350 degrees. Roll one portion of the dough at a time on a lightly floured surface 1/8 to 1/4 inch thick, keeping the remaining portion in the refrigerator. Cut with a 4- to 5-inch bird-shaped cookie cutter and place 1-inch apart on cookie sheets lined with baking parchment. Bake for 9 to 10 minutes or until the edges are light brown. (You want a very crisp cookie if you plan to glaze it.) Cool on the cookie sheets for 1 minute. Remove from the cookie sheets and cool completely.

To prepare the glaze, place a glass dish with a base large enough for a cookie to lay flat on the bottom into a larger container. Fill the outer container with hot water. Do not use boiling water. Break the chocolate into pieces. Place the chocolate and butter into the glass dish and stir until melted and smooth. (Be patient and let the chocolate melt completely.) Stir in the corn syrup and cherry liqueur. (You may add an additional tablespoon of cherry liqueur or milk if the glaze is not thin enough.) Replace the water in the outer container as need to keep the chocolate melted. (We do not recommend melting the chocolate in the microwave. Excessive heat will cause the chocolate to harden irreversibly.)

To glaze the cookies, using either your fingers or a fork, dip first the bottom and then the top of each cookie in the glaze and place on a rack over a tray to catch any excess glaze. Use a knife to smooth the surface of each cookie and to remove any excess glaze. Once the cookies have stopped dripping, move to a tray lined with waxed paper to dry.

Jacqulin Rognehaugh

To balance out the richness of the dark chocolate glaze, we reduced the sugar by half in the cookie dough. If you want a sweeter cookie, increase the sugar to 1 cup. Also, for a lighter tasting cookie, substitute semisweet or milk chocolate for the bittersweet chocolate. These cookies are also great served without the glaze.

Five Golden Rings

5

Gold holds great symbolic meaning during the holiday season. As we all know, gold was one of the three gifts that the Magi brought to celebrate the birth of Christ. The nativity scene is a common tradition for many when decorating the home for Christmas, and the scene almost always includes the three Magi bearing their gifts of gold, frankincense, and myrrh. Gold is also used as much as the traditional green and red colors when decorating the tree.

On a lighter note, our menu is quite down to earth today. We thought if your true love was saving up for a gold ring or two (or five!), they could save a buck or two by cooking a nice economical pulled pork sandwich. Or, if on this FIFTH DAY OF CHRISTMAS your true love happens to not have real gold on the menu, he or she can at least serve you our delicious Golden Brew Onion Rings.

Menu

Golden Ring Pulled Pork Sandwiches
Golden Brew Onion Rings
Thai Noodle Slaw
Creamy Potato Salad
Five-Ring Pineapple Upside-Down Cake

Cabernet / Zinfandel
We recommend:
AVELEDA Touriga Nacional—Cabernet sauvignon
Beiras Quinta d'Arguiera 2002
SOLARIS Zinfandel Napa Valley Special Release 2003

Today's Menu Serves Six

Golden Ring Pulled Pork Sandwiches

1 (4-pound) Boston butt pork roast
1/2 cup teriyaki sauce
1/2 cup vinegar
1 tablespoon dried minced onion
1 teaspoon dried minced garlic
1 teaspoon pepper
Melted butter for brushing (optional)
6 Golden Egg buns or soft Kaiser rolls
6 canned pineapple rings

Preheat the oven to 275 degrees. Place the pork in a large Dutch oven or large baking dish fitted with a lid. Mix the teriyaki sauce, vinegar, onion, garlic and pepper in a bowl. Pour over the pork. Cover the Dutch oven with a lid or tightly cover with foil. Bake for 4 hours or until the pork is tender and falls apart. Remove the pork from the Dutch oven to a cutting surface and let stand for 20 minutes or longer. Remove the string if the pork is tied and pull the pork apart into bite-size pieces either by hand or by using two forks, pulling the pork in opposite directions.

Preheat the broiler. Slightly hollow out the top side of each bun. Butter the cut side of the buns and place on a baking sheet. Broil until the buns are toasted. Butter the pineapple rings and place on a baking sheet. Broil for 5 minutes or until light brown, turning once.

To assemble the sandwiches, place the pulled pork on the bottom half of each bun. Top each with a pineapple slice and the bun top.

Golden Brew Onion Rings

1 cup all-purpose flour
2 tablespoons cornstarch
1/2 teaspoon garlic powder
1/4 teaspoon salt
2 teaspoons ground ginger (optional)
2 teaspoons sesame seeds (optional)
1 egg white, beaten
1 cup beer
Vegetable oil for frying
2 large Vidalia, Walla Walla or
other sweet onions, cut into 1/4-inch slices
and separated into rings

Mix the flour, cornstarch, garlic powder, salt, ginger and sesame seeds together in a shallow bowl. Stir in the egg white. Add the beer gradually, stirring constantly to form a thick batter and adding less or more beer to reach the desired consistency.

Pour 2 inches of oil into a large heavy skillet or deep fryer and heat over medium heat. Dip the onion rings into the batter. Fry in batches for 14 to 16 minutes or until golden brown, turning once. Remove from the oil with a slotted spoon and drain on paper towels. Serve immediately.

This batter can be used when deep-frying fish and other vegetables, such as bell peppers, zucchini, mushrooms, etc.

Thai Noodle Slaw

2 tablespoons peanut oil
3 tablespoons sesame oil
2 tablespoons soy sauce
3 tablespoons rice vinegar
2 garlic cloves, minced
1/2 tablespoon hot chile oil (optional)
1 (1-pound) package shredded cabbage with carrots
4 ounces fine egg noodles, cooked (Manischewitz brand was used for testing.)
1 (1-pound) package frozen peas, thawed
1/2 cup chopped green bell pepper
1/2 teaspoon minced jalapeño chile
1/4 cup chopped fresh cilantro

Whisk the peanut oil, sesame oil, soy sauce, vinegar, garlic and hot oil in a small bowl until blended. Combine the cabbage, noodles, peas, bell pepper, jalapeño chile and cilantro in a large bowl. Add the dressing and toss to coat.

Lisa Jensen

Creamy Potato Salad

5 large russet potatoes, peeled
5 cups water
1 teaspoon salt
1/2 cup mayonnaise (You may use low-fat; do not use fat-free.)
1/4 cup milk
2 tablespoons cider vinegar
2 tablespoons olive oil
1/2 teaspoon salt
1 teaspoon pepper
2 hard-cooked eggs, sliced
1/2 onion, minced
Chopped fresh parsley

Cut the potatoes into 1/2-inch slices. Cut each slice into quarters. Combine with water and 1 teaspoon salt in a large stockpot. Cover and bring to a boil. Reduce the heat and simmer for 8 to 10 minutes or until the potatoes are tender-crisp. Drain and rinse with cold water. Spoon into a serving bowl. Whisk the mayonnaise, milk, vinegar, olive oil, 1/2 teaspoon salt and the pepper in a small bowl until blended. Pour over the potatoes and mix gently with a wooden spoon. Fold in the eggs, onion and parsley.

Lisa Jensen

Five-Ring Pineapple Upside-Down Cake

1 (8-ounce) can sliced pineapple
3 tablespoons butter
1/2 cup packed brown sugar
4 maraschino cherries, cut into halves
1 cup sifted all-purpose flour
1 1/4 teaspoons baking powder
1/4 teaspoon salt
1/2 cup granulated sugar
1/3 cup safflower oil
1 egg
1 teaspoon vanilla extract

Preheat the oven to 350 degrees. Drain the pineapple, reserving the syrup. Melt the butter in an 8×8-inch baking dish. Stir in the brown sugar and 1 tablespoon of the reserved syrup. Arrange the pineapple in the prepared baking dish. Place a cherry half in the center of each ring cut side up.

Sift the flour, baking powder and salt together. Add enough water to the remaining pineapple syrup to measure 1/2 cup. Beat the sugar and safflower oil in a mixing bowl until light. Add the egg and vanilla and beat until fluffy. Add the flour mixture and pineapple syrup mixture alternately, beating well after each addition. Spread over the prepared pineapple layer. Bake for 40 to 45 minutes or until golden brown. Cool in the dish for 5 minutes and invert onto a serving plate. Serve warm.

Six Geese a Laying

Ah, the Christmas goose! I remember growing up as a child in Omaha, Nebraska, goose was the star attraction every Christmas Eve. Duck, however, gradually replaced the mighty goose as a less fatty alternative. Not that I'm complaining.

Goose is still the traditional Christmas main course throughout Europe. And we of course will never forget the part of Charles Dickens' A Christmas Carol *that elevated the place of goose at the table to a whole new level:*

"At last the dishes were set on, and grace was said. It was succeeded by a breathless pause, as Mrs. Cratchit, looking slowly all along the carving-knife, prepared to plunge it in the breast; but when she did, and when the long-expected gush of stuffing issued forth, one murmur of delight arose all round the board, and even Tiny Tim, excited by the two young Cratchits, beat on the table with the handle of his knife, and feebly cried, 'Hurrah! There never was such a goose.'"

But alas, since we have already included so many recipes featuring our foul friends within this cookbook, and since goose is not a particularly American tradition, we have devised a wonderful Six-Egg Frittata and a Gooseberry Fruit Tart to help you bring the goose into this SIXTH DAY OF CHRISTMAS.

Menu

Bruschetta
Mixed Greens Salad with Balsamic Vinaigrette
Six-Egg Frittata
Home Fries
Gooseberry Fruit Tart

Sauvignon Blanc / Pinot / Champagne
We recommend:
ZED Sauvignon Blanc Marlborough

Today's Menu Serves Four

Bruschetta

5 tablespoons extra-virgin olive oil
1 teaspoon minced fresh basil leaves
1 baguette, cut crosswise into 1-inch-thick slices
1 large garlic clove, peeled
Salt and pepper to taste

Preheat the broiler. Mix the olive oil and basil leaves in a bowl. Place the bread on a baking sheet. Broil until golden brown on each side, turning once. Rub the garlic over the toasted bread slices and brush with the olive oil mixture. Season with salt and pepper. Serve immediately.

Mixed Greens Salad with Balsamic Vinaigrette

1 1/2 teaspoons red wine vinegar
2 teaspoons balsamic vinegar
1/4 teaspoon salt
1/8 teaspoon pepper
3 tablespoons extra-virgin olive oil
1 pound mixed fresh salad greens,
rinsed and drained

Mix the red wine vinegar, balsamic vinegar, salt and pepper in a bowl. Add the olive oil and whisk or mix with a fork for 30 seconds. (The vinaigrette may be prepared in advance and refrigerated for up to one week. Mix the vinaigrette again before tossing with the salad greens.)

Pour the vinaigrette over the salad greens in a salad bowl and toss to coat.

Six-Egg Frittata

8 ounces Italian sausage or pancetta,
casings removed (optional)
1 small garlic clove, peeled and crushed
1 tablespoon extra-virgin olive oil
1 tablespoon minced fresh basil leaves
1 tablespoon minced fresh oregano leaves
1/4 cup sun-dried oil-pack tomatoes,
coarsely chopped
1/4 cup oil-cured olives, pitted and minced
6 eggs
1/3 cup shredded Gruyère cheese
1/4 teaspoon pepper

Preheat the oven to 350 degrees. Brown the sausage in a 12-inch cast-iron skillet; drain. Place the sausage in a bowl and set aside.

Sauté the garlic in the olive oil in the skillet over medium heat, removing the garlic from the skillet as it begins to color. Swirl the skillet to distribute the oil evenly over the bottom and side. Add the basil, oregano, sun-dried tomatoes and olives and stir to coat with the oil. Stir in the sausage. Spread in a single layer.

Beat the eggs lightly in a bowl. Stir in the cheese and pepper. Pour into the skillet. Cook over medium heat until the eggs begin to set, stirring lightly. Once the bottom is firm, use a thin spatula to lift the frittata edge closest to you. Tilt the skillet slightly towards you so that the uncooked eggs run underneath. Return the skillet to a level position and swirl gently to evenly distribute the egg mixture. Continue to cook for 40 seconds and lift the edge again, repeating the process until the egg mixture is no longer runny. Place the skillet on the upper middle rack in the oven. Bake for 2 to 4 minutes or until the top is set. Do not overcook. Run a spatula around the edge of the skillet to loosen the frittata and invert onto a serving dish. Serve warm, at room temperature or chilled.

Home Fries

1/2 cup minced sweet onion
3 tablespoons olive oil
4 potatoes, cooked and diced
Salt and pepper to taste

Sauté the onion in the olive oil in a 10-inch skillet over medium-high heat until tender. Add the potatoes and cook for 10 minutes or until brown, turning occasionally to ensure even browning. Season with salt and pepper.

Gooseberry Fruit Tart

Pastry

1 1/4 cups all-purpose flour
2 tablespoons sugar
1/8 teaspoon salt
1/8 teaspoon baking powder
6 tablespoons unsalted butter, chilled and cut into 1/2-inch pieces
1 egg
1 tablespoon water

Tart

3 tablespoons sugar
2 tablespoons all-purpose flour
Pinch of salt
3/4 cup milk
1 egg
1 egg yolk
1 teaspoon vanilla extract
1 tablespoon unsalted butter, softened
2 teaspoons orange liqueur or Kirsch
1 (15-ounce) can gooseberries in light syrup
1 teaspoon sugar
1/8 teaspoon ground cinnamon

To prepare the pastry, mix the flour, sugar, salt and baking powder in a food processor fitted with a steel blade. Scatter the butter pieces over the flour mixture and pulse until the mixture resembles coarse cornmeal. Spoon into a medium bowl. Beat the egg and 1 tablespoon water with a fork in a bowl. Fold the egg mixture into the flour mixture until the dough sticks together and forms a ball. (You may add up to another 1 tablespoon water if the dough does not come together.) Shape the dough into a ball, squeezing two or three times with your hands to form a cohesive dough. Flatten the ball into a 4-inch disk and wrap in plastic wrap. Chill for at least 1 hour or up to 2 days before rolling.

Preheat the oven to 400 degrees. Remove the dough from the refrigerator and let stand at room temperature for 15 minutes or until the dough is soft and pliable. (The dough is ready to roll if you can squeeze it without having to apply too much pressure.) Roll the dough 1/8 inch thick on a lightly floured piece of baking parchment. Fit into eight individual tart cups, fluting the edge by pressing the thumb and index finger of one hand about 1/2 inch apart and pinching the dough at 1/2-inch intervals. (You may also fit the dough into a 12-inch tart pan, or slide the parchment paper and dough onto a baking sheet, fold up 1/2-inch around the perimeter of the disk and flute the edge.) Place on the center oven rack and reduce the oven temperature to 350 degrees. Bake for 20 minutes or until golden brown. Cool in the tart pans on a wire rack.

To prepare the tart, whisk 3 tablespoons sugar, flour and salt together in a 1- to 1 1/2-quart nonreactive saucepan. Whisk in the milk until smooth. Whisk in the egg and egg yolk until smooth. Cook over low heat until the mixture thickens and comes to a boil, whisking constantly. Boil for 15 seconds, whisking constantly. Remove from the heat and whisk in the vanilla and butter until smooth. Spoon into a nonreactive bowl and press plastic wrap against the surface. Chill for 1 to 12 hours. Remove the plastic wrap and stir in the liqueur. Spread evenly into the tart shells.

Drain the gooseberries, reserving the liquid. Combine the reserved liquid, 1 teaspoon sugar and the cinnamon in a bowl and blend well. Fold in the gooseberries. Spoon over the top of the tarts and serve immediately.

7 Seven Swans a Swimming

If your true love were to give you Swans a Swimming on this SEVENTH DAY OF CHRISTMAS he or she would be proclaiming a life-long love. Swans, you see, mate for life. And oddly enough, there are exactly seven types of swans: Whooper, Trumpeter, Tundra, Mute, Black-necked, Black and Coscoroba. Maybe you will get one of each this Christmas season!

Through the years, swans have represented the grace and beauty of a woman, such as in the enchanting ballet Swan Lake. *May our light and delicate Swan Lake Tilapia and Swan Cream Puffs add grace and beauty to your table this holiday season or any time of the year.*

Menu

Swan Dive Endive
Swan Lake Tilapia
Vegetable Couscous
Swan Cream Puffs

Sauvignon Blanc / Pinot
We rcommend:
Matua Valley Pinot Noir 2004

Today's Menu Serves Four

Swan Dive Endive

1 (3-ounce) jar of small Spanish olives
1 cup garbanzo beans, rinsed and drained
1 tomato, finely chopped
1 teaspoon olive oil
1 teaspoon balsamic vinegar
8 large Belgian endive leaves, or
12 small endive leaves, rinsed
1 avocado, diced (optional)
Crumbled feta cheese (optional)

Drain the olives and cut into halves. Combine the olives, beans, tomato, olive oil and vinegar in a small bowl and toss to mix. Arrange two large endive leaves on each of four salad plates. Place 3 tablespoons of the bean mixture inside each of the eight leaves. (If you are using small endive leaves, place three leaves in a fan arrangement per plate and add 2 tablespoons of the bean mixture inside each of the twelve leaves. (You may make ahead the same day up to this point and chill in the refrigerator.) Sprinkle evenly with the avocado and feta cheese just before serving.

Lisa Jensen

Swan Lake Tilapia

Piccata Sauce
1 cup chicken broth
1/4 cup white wine
1 tablespoon lemon juice
1 tablespoon capers
2 tablespoons butter
2 tablespoons all-purpose flour
1/2 tablespoon minced garlic

Tilapia
4 tilapia fillets
1/4 cup white wine
1 tablespoon capers
2 tablespoons lemon juice
1 teaspoon olive oil
1/4 tablespoon kosher salt
1/4 tablespoon pepper
1/4 cup bread crumbs

Sautéed Spinach
1 (6-ounce) package baby spinach
1 teaspoon olive oil
Squeeze of lemon juice
Salt and pepper to taste

To prepare the sauce, combine the broth, wine, lemon juice and capers in a small bowl and mix well. Melt the butter in a small saucepan over medium-low heat. Whisk in the flour and garlic. Cook for 10 minutes, whisking frequently. (This is to remove the raw flour taste and it is okay if the mixture browns a bit.) Whisk in the broth mixture gradually to ensure lumps do not form. Boil for 1 minute or until thickened, whisking constantly. (The sauce can be made slightly ahead and reheated, if desired.)

To prepare the fish, preheat the oven to 350 degrees. Place the fish in a 9×13-inch baking pan. Mix the wine, capers, lemon juice and olive oil in a small bowl and pour over the fish. Sprinkle the fish evenly with kosher salt and pepper. Sprinkle evenly with the bread crumbs. Bake, uncovered, for 25 minutes or until the fish flakes easily with a fork.

To prepare the spinach, sauté the spinach in the olive oil in a large skillet over medium heat for 15 to 20 seconds. Add the lemon juice and sauté for 15 to 20 seconds. Season with salt and pepper.

To serve, place equal amounts of the spinach on four plates and top each with one fish fillet. Spoon the desired amount of sauce over the top.

Lisa Jensen

Vegetable Couscous

2/3 cup chopped zucchini
2/3 cup chopped yellow squash
1/2 cup chopped red bell pepper
1/2 teaspoon lemon pepper
1 teaspoon olive oil
1 (5-ounce) package of Parmesan-flavored couscous
(Near East brand was used for testing.)

Sauté the zucchini, squash, bell pepper and lemon pepper in the olive oil in a medium skillet over medium-high heat for 3 minutes. Cover and remove from the heat.

Cook the couscous in a saucepan using the package directions. Stir in the sautéed vegetables and serve immediately.

Lisa Jensen

Swan Cream Puffs

1/2 cup (1 stick) butter
1 cup boiling water
1/4 teaspoon salt
1 cup sifted all-purpose flour
3 or 4 eggs
Filling Variations (*See* page 55.)

Combine the butter, boiling water and salt in a 2-quart saucepan. Heat just until the mixture comes to a boil and remove from the heat. Add the flour all at once, stirring vigorously until the mixture forms a ball and separates from the side of the pan. Add the eggs one at a time, blending well after each addition until the dough is smooth. (If your eggs are large, you may need to add only three. Your batter should be soft enough to go through a pastry tip, but firm enough to form mounds for the body. The batter should not be runny.) Let the mixture cool slightly.

Preheat the oven to 375 degrees. Lightly grease two baking sheets or line with baking parchment. Fill a pastry bag fitted with a 5/8-inch rose tip with 1/2 cup of the dough. Pipe twelve to fourteen S-shaped swan necks onto one of the prepared baking sheets. (Extra necks provide for possible breakage.) Drop heaping tablespoonfuls of the remaining dough into 2-inch long oval mounds to create twelve to fourteen swan bodies onto the remaining prepared baking sheet, leaving room for the mounds to expand. Bake for 10 minutes or until the swan necks are golden on the bottom. Remove the swan necks from the oven. Continue to bake the swan bodies for 15 to 20 minutes longer or until golden on the bottom. Remove from the oven. Let stand for 1 hour at room temperature before assembling and filling (See photograph page 108). Fill the swans with the desired filling no more than 1 to 2 hours before serving. (The baked swan bodies and necks can be frozen in an airtight container for several weeks. Thaw for 1 hour at room temperature before filling. Freezing can soften the texture of the puffs.)

Filling Variations:

To prepare **Vanilla Cream Filling**, prepare a 3-ounce package of vanilla pudding and pie filling mix using the package directions. Cover the surface with plastic wrap and chill for about 2 hours. Beat 1 cup heavy whipping cream at medium speed in a small mixing bowl until stiff peaks form. Using a rubber spatula, fold gently into the pudding.

To prepare **Almond Cream Filling**, prepare the Vanilla Cream Filling as above, adding 1 teaspoon almond extract.

For **White Swans**, fill the puffs with one scoop of vanilla ice cream per swan and store in the freezer until ready to serve.

For **Black Swans**, fill the puffs with one scoop of chocolate ice cream per swan and drizzle the body of the swan with melted semisweet chocolate. Store in the freezer until ready to serve.

Eight Maids a Milking

This EIGHTH DAY OF CHRISTMAS takes us back to the dairy states. All four writers of this cookbook are from a lovely city situated in the middle of the country—Omaha, Nebraska. We keep to a real midwestern theme today with ingredients such as sour cream, whipping cream, and ice cream. The grandfather of one of our writers owned a dairy farm in Omaha at the intersection of 72nd and Dodge way before there were any streets or roads around for miles. The land was later sold, but his son Kenneth kept part of the farm and opened a small restaurant called the Green Gables. He soon renamed the restaurant Kenny's, and it became one of the best steak houses in town. We hope you enjoy our very dairy menu. Let's not count calories today, and just keep those maid's a milking!

Menu

Creamy Onion Dressing with Tossed Greens Salad
Sweet Potato Fries
Milkmaid Sandwiches
Black Cow Milk Shakes
Baggie Ice Cream

Vouvray
We recommend:
BENOIT GAUTIER Vouvray 2004

Today's Menu Serves Four

Creamy Onion Dressing

1 cup heavy whipping cream
2 tablespoons lemon juice
1/4 teaspoon salt
Dash of white pepper
Dash of cayenne pepper
3/4 cup minced green onions

Whip the whipping cream lightly in a bowl. Stir in the lemon juice gradually. Season with the salt, white pepper and cayenne pepper. Stir in the green onions. Serve over your favorite salad greens.

Sweet Potato Fries

Vegetable oil for deep-frying
1 pound sweet potatoes
1 tablespoon butter or margarine, melted
1/4 teaspoon seasoned salt
Dash of ground nutmeg

Heat the oil in a deep fryer using the manufacturer's directions. (For stovetop frying, heat 2 inches of oil in a skillet over medium-high heat.) Cut the sweet potatoes into thin or chunky strips. Carefully drop the sweet potatoes into the oil. Deep-fry until the sweet potatoes rise to the surface and are golden. Remove with a slotted spoon to paper towels to drain. Season with salt and nutmeg.

Milkmaid Sandwiches

1/2 onion, minced
1 tablespoon vegetable oil
1 pound ground beef
1/2 cup chopped fresh mushrooms
1/4 teaspoon salt
Dash of pepper
1/4 to 1/2 cup beef broth or water
1/4 cup sour cream (optional)
Butter to taste
4 hamburger buns
Dill pickle slices

Sauté the onion in the oil in a large skillet over medium-low heat until lightly caramelized. Add the ground beef. Cook until brown, using a potato masher or wooden spoon to chop the ground beef into fine, rice-size pieces. Add the mushrooms. Sauté for 5 minutes; drain. Season with salt and pepper. Sauté over low heat for 5 minutes, adding enough of the broth to maintain a moist (but not runny) consistency. Stir in the sour cream and remove from the heat.

Preheat the broiler. Spread butter over the cut sides of the buns and place on a baking sheet. Broil until the buns are toasted. To serve, spoon 1/2 cup of the ground beef mixture on the bottom half of each bun. Top with pickles and the top half of each bun.

Black Cow Milk Shakes

1 pint dark chocolate ice cream
1 pint vanilla ice cream
3 tablespoons chocolate malt milk powder
1 cup chilled root beer

Blend the chocolate ice cream, vanilla ice cream, malt milk powder and root beer at high speed in a blender until smooth. Divide the mixture evenly between four 8-ounce glasses. Garnish with whipped cream and maraschino cherries. Serve with a straw and iced tea spoon.

Baggie Ice Cream

1/2 cup milk
1/2 cup heavy whipping cream
1/4 cup sugar
1 teaspoon vanilla extract
2 cups ice
1/4 cup rock salt

Combine the milk, cream, sugar and vanilla in a 1-quart sealable plastic bag. Seal the bag and shake to mix. Place the sealed bag inside a 1-gallon sealable plastic bag. Add the ice and rock salt to the large bag and seal. Toss or shake the bags gently for 15 minutes or until firm. (Have the kids play catch.) Voilà! You have ice cream! (For variety, use flavored milk or creamers.)

Jean Osborn

Nine Ladies Dancing

I cannot think of a better way to celebrate any occasion than by kicking up your heels and doing a little dancing. During Mardi Gras, Cajun women are known to do a little dance to put the children to sleep called the Happy Fais do do (pronounced Happy Fay doe doe) which is a bit of gibberish that some say is Cajun baby talk meaning "make-sleep-sleep". What this all has to do with the NINTH DAY OF CHRISTMAS, well, we don't really know. But what we "do do" know is that we love Cajun food and needed an excuse to incorporate some fantastic recipes such as Alligator Stomp Artichokes, Dancing Shrimp Creole, and Maque Choux (pronounced "make shoo").

We would like to offer up a special remembrance to Jeanne Wade who was the inspiration for both the artichokes and creole.

Menu

Alligator Stomp Artichokes
Dancing Shrimp Creole
Maque Choux
Miniature Corn on the Cob
Crusty French Bread
Bananas Foster
Pecan Pie
Basic Gingerbread Cookies

Sauvignon Blanc / Dry Reisling
We recommend:
REILLY'S Riesling Clare Valley Barking Mad 2004

Today's Menu Serves Six

Alligator Stomp Artichokes

3 fresh artichokes (allow 1/2 per person)
1 teaspoon salt
1 cup Italian bread crumbs
1/4 teaspoon cayenne pepper
1/2 teaspoon paprika
1/2 teaspoon oregano
3 tablespoons butter, melted

Cut off the artichoke stems evenly so the artichokes can sit upright in a baking dish. Place the artichokes in a large saucepan and add enough water to partially cover. (The artichokes will float.) Sprinkle with the salt. Bring to a boil and reduce the heat. Cover and simmer for 45 minutes. Remove the artichokes with large tongs, turning each upside down to drain the water from each one. Place the artichokes upright in a large baking dish and let stand until cool. With your fingers, gently spread the leaves apart but keep them intact.

Preheat the oven to 350 degrees. Mix the bread crumbs, cayenne pepper, paprika and oregano in a bowl. With a small spoon, sprinkle the bread crumb mixture evenly over the artichokes, making sure the bread crumb mixture gets down into the leaves to create a coating on each leaf. Pour the melted butter into a measuring cup or gravy boat that has a spout. Drizzle the butter evenly over the leaves. Bake for 15 to 20 minutes.

To eat, pull off one artichoke leaf at a time and scrape off the artichoke meat and coating with your teeth. Discard the leaf. As you get to the center, the artichoke heart can be eaten as well, but be sure to remove the feathery "choke."

Lisa Jensen

Dancing Shrimp Creole

1/4 cup vegetable oil
1/4 cup all-purpose flour
1 1/2 cups chopped onions
1 cup chopped celery
3/4 cup sliced green onions
1 large green bell pepper, chopped
1/2 jalapeño chile, minced
2 garlic cloves, minced
1 (15-ounce) can diced tomatoes
1 (6-ounce) can tomato paste
1 cup water
3 bay leaves
1/2 teaspoon dried thyme
1 teaspoon cayenne pepper
1 teaspoon paprika
1/2 teaspoon dried oregano
1/2 teaspoon salt
1/2 teaspoon black pepper
1 tablespoon lemon juice
2 teaspoons Worcestershire sauce
4 dashes (or more) of Tabasco sauce or your favorite hot red pepper sauce
1 to 4 pounds fresh medium shrimp, peeled and deveined
2 tablespoons chopped fresh parsley
Hot cooked rice

Cook the oil and flour in a large stockpot or Dutch oven over medium heat for 15 minutes or until the mixture is golden brown, stirring constantly. Add the onions, celery, green onions, bell pepper, jalapeño chile and garlic. Cook for 15 minutes, stirring frequently. Stir in the undrained tomatoes, tomato paste and water. Add the bay leaves, thyme, cayenne pepper, paprika, oregano, salt, black pepper, lemon juice, Worcestershire sauce and Tabasco sauce. Bring to a boil and reduce the heat. Cover and simmer for 1 hour, stirring occasionally. Add the shrimp. Simmer for 10 minutes or until the shrimp turn pink. Remove the bay leaves. Stir in the parsley. Serve over hot cooked rice.

Lisa Jensen and Mark Armstrong

Maque Choux

12 ears of corn, shucked, or
1 (16-ounce) package frozen corn
1 onion, finely chopped
2 tablespoons butter
1/2 green bell pepper, chopped
2 tablespoons chopped tomato
2 tablespoons chopped green chiles
Salt and pepper to taste

Cut the corn from the cob into a bowl. Sauté the onion in the butter in a heavy saucepan until the onion is slightly caramelized. Stir in the corn, bell pepper, tomato, green chiles, salt and pepper. Cook over low heat for 20 to 30 minutes or until the corn is tender, stirring frequently.

Bananas Foster

6 small ripe bananas
Lemon juice
1 cup packed brown sugar
1/4 cup (1/2 stick) butter
Dash of ground cinnamon
1/4 cup rum
Vanilla ice cream

Peel the bananas and cut into halves lengthwise. Brush each half with lemon juice to prevent discoloration. Heat the brown sugar and butter in a skillet over medium heat until melted. Add the bananas and cinnamon. Cook, uncovered, for 3 minutes.

Heat the rum in a small saucepan until just warm. Remove the saucepan from the heat. Ignite the rum and let the flames subside. Pour over the banana mixture. Serve over ice cream in dessert bowls.

Pecan Pie

3 eggs
1/4 cup (1/2 stick) butter, melted
1 cup dark corn syrup
1/2 cup packed brown sugar
1/4 teaspoon ground cinnamon
1 cup pecan halves
1 unbaked (9-inch) pie shell

Preheat the oven to 350 degrees. Whisk the eggs in a medium bowl. Add the butter, corn syrup, brown sugar and cinnamon and beat until blended. Fold in the pecan halves. Pour into the pie shell, making sure the pecans are evenly distributed on the surface of the pie. Bake for 1 hour or until a knife inserted in the center comes out clean. Cool on a wire rack before serving.

Jacqulin Rognehaugh

You can painstakingly arrange the pecans on the bottom of the pie shell if you want. I find that they are difficult to keep from floating where they want any way. Besides, the random order can be just as visually interesting.

Basic Gingerbread Cookies

1/2 cup shortening or 1/2 cup (1 stick) butter
1/2 cup molasses
1 egg
1/2 cup sugar
2 cups all-purpose flour
1/2 teaspoon baking soda
1 teaspoon baking powder
1 teaspoon ground cinnamon
1 teaspoon ground ginger
1 teaspoon ground cloves
1/4 teaspoon salt

Beat the shortening, molasses and egg at medium speed in a large mixing bowl until blended. Add the sugar, flour, baking soda, baking powder, cinnamon, ginger, cloves and salt and mix well. Cover the dough and chill for 3 hours.

Preheat the oven to 350 degrees. Grease the cookie sheets or line with baking parchment. Roll the chilled dough 1/8 inch thick with a rolling pin on a lightly floured surface. Cut half the dough with a gingerbread lady cookie cutter. Cut the remaining half of the dough with a gingerbread man cookie cutter. Place 1/2-inch apart on the prepared cookie sheets. (You can make your gingerbread ladies dance and gingerbread men leap by carefully moving their arms, legs and bodies into different positions.) Bake for 6 to 7 minutes or until brown. Cool slightly on the cookie sheets. Remove to a wire rack to cool completely.

Ten Lords a Leaping

Today's menu has a very British theme with Lords of London Broil, Duchess Potatoes, and Chocolate Orange "Royale" cakes, which is very fitting as the Twelve Days of Christmas song is believed to have originated in England. The Lords a Leaping that are referred to on this TENTH DAY OF CHRISTMAS *are believed to represent poor minstrels who would perform on the streets for money. They may have gone door to door during the Christmas season, similar to the European tradition of wassailing. By the way, the term wassail means "be in good health." Using wassail as a toast actually began in Denmark, however the British took the idea to it's current tradition of walking through the streets caroling and wishing good fortune to others. The recipients serve the wassail drink and hearty fare to cheer on the wassailer. Americans, of course, take this concept to a whole new level as we cheer on our favorite football teams all through December. I bet the lords of England never leapt like that!*

Menu

Savory Popovers
Lords of London Broil
Duchess Potatoes
House of Lords Brussels Sprouts
Chocolate Orange Royale Cakes

Cabernet
We recommend:
The Long Paddock Shiraz Cabernet Sauvignon 2003

Today's Menu Serves Six

Savory Popovers

1 cup all-purpose flour
1/4 teaspoon salt
1 cup milk
2 extra-large eggs
1 tablespoon butter, melted

Preheat the oven to 450 degrees. Preheat twelve empty muffin cups on the lowest oven rack. Whisk the flour and salt together in a medium bowl. Whisk the milk, eggs and butter in a large measuring cup with a pour spout. Whisk in the flour mixture until blended. Remove the muffin cups from the oven and lightly grease each cup and rim. Fill each cup half-full with the batter. Bake for 20 minutes. Do not open the oven door. Reduce the oven temperature to 350 degrees. Bake for 15 to 20 minutes longer or until the popovers are rich brown in color. Serve warm.

Variations:

For **Herb Popovers**, add 1 teaspoon crushed fresh herbs (1/4 teaspoon dried herbs), such as rosemary, thyme, chives or oregano to the batter.

For **Cheesy Popovers**, add shredded asiago cheese or Cheddar cheese to taste to the batter.

Lords of London Broil

1 (3-pound) London Broil cut of beef (top sirloin roast), about 2 inches thick (Make sure the London Broil is a good cut of beef as it can be tough if not of good quality.)
1 cup red wine
3 garlic cloves, crushed
1/2 tablespoon black pepper
1/2 teaspoon red pepper
1/2 teaspoon kosher salt
1/4 cup of your favorite barbecue sauce
1/4 cup soy sauce
1 tablespoon Tabasco jalapeño green pepper sauce or your favorite hot green pepper sauce

Place the beef in a large sealable plastic bag. Mix the wine, garlic, black pepper, red pepper, kosher salt, barbecue sauce, soy sauce and Tabasco sauce in a bowl. Pour over the beef and seal the bag. Marinate in the refrigerator for 24 hours.

Place the baking rack in the highest position in the oven and preheat the broiler. Spray the rack of a broiler pan with cooking spray. Drain the beef, discarding the marinade. Place the beef on the prepared rack in a broiler pan. Bake, with the oven door slightly ajar, for 6 1/2 minutes per side for medium-rare. Remove from the oven and let stand for 15 minutes. Cut into slices against the grain. Serve immediately.

Mark Armstrong

Duchess Potatoes

3 cups water
1 teaspoon salt
3 russet potatoes, peeled and cut into 1-inch pieces
1/2 cup beef broth
1 tablespoon butter
1/2 teaspoon dried minced garlic
1/4 cup (1 ounce) grated Parmesan cheese
1/2 teaspoon tarragon
1/2 teaspoon salt
1/2 teaspoon pepper
1 egg yolk

Combine the water and 1 teaspoon salt in a medium stockpot. Cover and bring to a boil. Add the potatoes carefully and cook at a low boil for 15 minutes or until very tender. Drain the potatoes and return to the stockpot. Add 1/4 cup of the broth and the butter and mash using a potato masher or electric mixer until smooth. Add the remaining 1/4 cup broth if needed to reach the desired consistency. Add the garlic, Parmesan cheese, tarragon, 1/2 teaspoon salt, the pepper and egg yolk and mash until thoroughly mixed.

Preheat the oven to 450 degrees. Spray a baking sheet with nonstick cooking spray. Mound the mashed potatoes in eight separate mounds on the prepared baking sheet. Bake for 10 to 15 minutes or until light brown.

Lisa Jensen

House of Lords Brussels Sprouts

1 tablespoon butter
1/4 cup (scant) Italian bread crumbs
1 pound fresh brussels sprouts, or 1 (16-ounce) package frozen brussels sprouts, thawed and cut into halves
Salt and pepper to taste

Melt the butter in a 12-inch skillet over medium heat. Add the bread crumbs and mix well. Add the brussels sprouts and toss to coat. Cook for 12 minutes or until the brussels sprouts are tender and heated through and the bread crumbs are toasted. Season with salt and pepper.

This recipe is adapted from Land O' Lakes Saucy-Center Mocha Cakes.

Chocolate Orange Royale Cakes

6 tablespoons butter
1 cup (6 ounces) semisweet chocolate chips
2 teaspoons instant coffee granules
3 eggs
1/2 cup granulated sugar
2 tablespoons all-purpose flour
1/4 teaspoon (scant) ground cloves
1/2 teaspoon orange extract
1 teaspoon coarsely grated or chopped fresh orange peel
Confectioners' sugar
Coarsely shredded or chopped fresh orange peel
Chopped pistachio nuts
Whipped cream

Preheat the oven to 400 degrees. Grease and lightly flour six glass custard cups. Place on an ungreased baking sheet. Melt the butter, chocolate chips and coffee granules in a 1-quart saucepan over medium heat, stirring occasionally. Cook for 2 to 3 minutes or until smooth, stirring occasionally. Set aside.

Beat the eggs at high speed in a small mixing bowl until slightly thick and pale yellow. Add the sugar gradually, beating constantly until light and fluffy. Add the chocolate mixture, flour, cloves, orange extract and 1 teaspoon orange peel and beat at low speed until mixed. Pour equal amounts into the prepared custard cups. Bake for 11 to 13 minutes or until the tops are puffy and cracked in appearance but the centers are still soft. Cool for 5 minutes. Loosen the side of each cake with a knife and invert onto individual serving plates. Sprinkle with confectioners' sugar, coarsely shredded orange peel and pistachio nuts. Serve warm with whipped cream, if desired.

The batter can be prepared several hours ahead. Bake just before serving. Cover and refrigerate if more than 1 hour. Allow to stand at room temperature for at least 15 minutes to warm slightly before baking. (We found that the batter needed to stand at room temperature for 30 minutes before baking.)

Eleven Pipers Piping

11

Today we honor a very special Canadian tradition for this ELEVENTH DAY OF CHRISTMAS. Tourtière is a wonderful meat pie that is traditionally served throughout Canada after the Christmas Eve midnight mass. If you celebrate the Twelve Days of Christmas prior to Christmas, starting on December 14th, then today is Christmas Eve! Tourtiere is usually made with ground pork, onions, and mushrooms, and wrapped in crusts that cover both the bottom and top of the pie. It is usually served with ketchup and pickles, and so to follow that theme, we feature a delicious Fresh Tomato Bisque and a platter of assorted pickled appetizers. No matter what country you are from, we hope you try our French Canadian menu this Christmas Eve.

We give special thanks to Olive Armstrong from Toronto, Canada, for sharing her version of the tourtière.

Menu

Peter Piper Pickled Platter
Marinated Artichokes and Mushrooms
Fresh Tomato Bisque
Piping Hot Pork Pie (French Canadian Tourtière)
Cranberry Compote

Pinot Grigio / Australian Chardonnay (not oak)
We recommend:
Naked Chardonnay, Four Vines, Santa Barbara County 2004
TENUTA ANSELMI Pinot Grigio Latisana del Friuli

Today's Menu Serves Six

Peter Piper Pickled Platter

1 (12-ounce) jar pepperoncini
1 (12-ounce) jar dilled green beans
1 (8-ounce) jar marinated mushrooms
1 (6-ounce) jar marinated artichokes
1 (15-ounce) can cannellini
1 tablespoon olive oil (optional)
1 tablespoon balsamic vinegar (optional)

Arrange the chiles, green beans, mushrooms, artichokes and beans in columns on a large platter. Drizzle with olive oil and balsamic vinegar.

Lisa Jensen

This recipe can be used in the Peter Piper Pickled Platter above.

Marinated Artichokes and Mushrooms

1/2 cup red wine vinegar
1/2 cup extra-light olive oil
2 green onions, thinly sliced
1 teaspoon mustard
1 tablespoon brown sugar
2 teaspoons dried oregano
2 teaspoons dried parsley
1 (15-ounce) can quartered artichoke hearts, drained
2 (6-ounce) cans button mushrooms, drained

Combine the vinegar, olive oil, green onions, mustard, brown sugar, oregano and parsley in a medium saucepan. Bring to a boil over medium heat. Add the artichoke hearts and mushrooms. Return to a boil and reduce the heat. Simmer for 5 minutes. Place in a covered container. Marinate, covered, in the refrigerator for 3 hours or longer, stirring occasionally.

Traditionally the French and Canadians would serve their tourtière with ketchup. We have put our own twist on the menu with Jean Osborn's Fresh Tomato Bisque.

Fresh Tomato Bisque

4 cups water
4 pounds tomatoes
1 onion, chopped
3 tablespoons butter
2 tablespoons all-purpose flour
2 cups chicken broth
2 tablespoons brown sugar
6 cloves
1 teaspoon salt, or to taste
1 teaspoon freshly ground pepper, or to taste
1/2 to 1 cup whipping cream

Bring the water to a boil in a large Dutch oven or stockpot. Cut an X in the bottom of each tomato. Place the tomatoes (in batches if needed) in the boiling water. Boil for 5 minutes or until the skins begin to peel; drain. Remove the tomatoes with tongs and place in a large bowl. Let stand for 10 minutes or until cool.

Sauté the onion in the butter in the Dutch oven over medium heat for 10 minutes or until tender and brown. Sprinkle with the flour. Cook until the mixture begins to foam, stirring constantly. Add the broth and bring to a boil, stirring constantly. Remove from the heat and set aside.

Peel the cooled tomatoes and place on a work surface. Coarsely chop the tomatoes, discarding the seeds. Reserve 3/4 cup of the chopped tomatoes. Add the remaining tomatoes to the onion broth. Stir in the brown sugar, cloves, salt and pepper. Bring to a boil and reduce the heat. Simmer for 30 minutes. Remove the Dutch oven from the heat. Pour the tomato mixture into a large bowl and let stand until cool. Purée in batches using a food mill, food processor or blender, returning the puréed tomatoes to the Dutch oven. Stir in the reserved 3/4 cup chopped tomatoes. Stir in enough of the cream to suit your taste. Gently heat over medium heat. Do not boil. Ladle into soup bowls.

Jean Osborn

Alors, c'est magnifique!

Piping Hot Pork Pie (French Canadian Tourtière)

Pastry
2 1/4 cups all-purpose flour
1/2 teaspoon salt
2 tablespoons butter
3/4 cup shortening
5 tablespoons water

Pie
2 pounds ground pork
3 small onions, finely chopped (use a food processor if available)
1 cup finely chopped celery (use a food processor if available)
6 garlic cloves, crushed and finely chopped
2 cups thinly sliced button mushrooms
1/4 teaspoon salt
Pinch of ground cloves
1/2 teaspoon ground cinnamon
1/2 teaspoon savory
1/2 teaspoon cayenne pepper
1 1/4 cups beef broth
1 cup plain bread crumbs
1/2 cup chopped fresh parsley
1 egg
1 teaspoon water

To prepare the pastry, sift the flour and salt together into a bowl. Cut in the butter and shortening using a potato masher, adding the water 1 tablespoon at a time until the mixture resembles small peas. Chill in the refrigerator for 15 minutes.

To prepare the pie, brown the ground pork in a large skillet, stirring until crumbly. Mash with a potato masher to break up the ground pork into very small granular pieces; drain. Stir in the onions, celery, garlic, mushrooms, salt, cloves, cinnamon, savory, cayenne pepper and broth. Simmer for 45 minutes or until there is only about 2 tablespoons of liquid remaining, stirring frequently. Stir in the bread crumbs and parsley. Remove from the heat to cool.

Remove the pastry from the refrigerator. Roll the pastry with a floured rolling pin 1/8 inch thick on a lightly floured surface. Place a 10-inch pie plate upside down in the middle of the pastry. (There should be a lot of pastry remaining around the edge.) Cut around the circumference of the dish with a sharp knife, adding an extra 1/4 inch around to account for the side of the pie plate. Reserve all of the remaining pastry. Remove the pie plate from the pastry and spray the pie plate lightly with cooking spray. Carefully fit the cutout piece of pastry in the pie plate and use your fingers or a fork to press or flute the edge.

Shape the reserved remaining pastry into a ball. Roll the pastry with a floured rolling pin 1/8 inch thick on a lightly floured work surface. Set aside. Whisk the egg and 1 teaspoon water in a small dish until blended.

Place the ground pork mixture in the prepared pie plate, spreading evenly and pressing down to form a dense mixture. Brush the edges of the pastry with the egg mixture. Place the pastry circle over the top, using your fingers or a fork to press or flute the edges together. Brush with the remaining egg mixture to ensure a nice brown crust. (If there are any pieces of pastry remaining, tradition has been for the children to make shapes of Christmas decorations and place them on top of the pie.)

Preheat the oven to 375 degrees. Bake the pie for 45 minutes. Remove from the oven and let stand for 15 minutes or until cool. Cut into 2-inch slices to serve. Garnish with ketchup or spicy tomato sauce.

Olive Armstrong

Cranberry Compote

1 cup water
1/2 to 3/4 cup sugar
1 teaspoon lemon juice
1 (12-ounce) package cranberries, or
1 (6-ounce) package dried cranberry/cherry mix
1/4 cup crystallized ginger
Vanilla ice cream

Combine the water, sugar and lemon juice in a medium saucepan. Cook over low heat until the sugar dissolves, stirring occasionally. Increase the heat and bring the mixture to a boil. Add the cranberries. Return to a boil and reduce the heat. Simmer for 5 to 7 minutes or until the cranberries begin to pop. Stir in the ginger. Pour into a nonaluminum container. Cover and chill in the refrigerator. Spoon over ice cream to serve.

Twelve Drummers Drumming

12

For those of you that begin your Twelve Days of Christmas celebration on December 14th, then today is the day we have all been counting down to—Christmas Day has finally arrived! What a wonderfully fitting way to celebrate the TWELFTH DAY OF CHRISTMAS*! Bring on the great and mighty drum roll! Let the drummers sound out the crescendo of the holiday season with snares, tom toms, kettles, and cymbals!*

MERRY CHRISTMAS!

Christmas Day traditions are as varied as our fingerprints, but one common theme we hear frequently is the "Open House" concept where a variety of appetizers, salads, main dishes, and desserts are prepared to be presented throughout the day as guests come and go.

We hope you enjoy our Drummers Drumming Open House menu!

Menu

Appetizers

Spicy Drummettes

Swan Dive Endive (page 52)

Shrimp-Stuffed Baby Bellas

Stilton Cheese Appetizer

Cranberry and Brie Canapés

Crab and Asiago Cheese Dip

Fresh Vegetable Platter

Salads and Side Dishes

Grilled Asparagus Spears

Southern Praline Yams

Rosemary Dijon Potatoes

Wild Rice Salad with Cranberries

Main Dishes

Madeira-Glazed Turkey Breast

Spicy Flank Steak with Corn and Pepper Salsa

Grilled Salmon

Cider Vinegar-Glazed Ham

Desserts

Pear Gallette

Fresh Raspberry Cheesecake

Chocolate Peppermint Roll

Lemon Pound Cake

Kings Cake Cupcakes

Beverages

Coffee and Tea

Variety of Champagnes, Pinot Noir or Burgundy

We recommend:

CASTLE ROCK Pinot Noir
Monterey County 2004

Today's Menu Serves
Approximately Fifty

Preparing for an open house spread can be an overwhelming task. We offer all of these recipes for you to pick and choose from depending on the number of your guests. If you were to make this entire spread, it would serve approximately fifty guests. Here are some suggestions to help organize your preparation. These suggestions are for if you would like to serve everything cool or at room temperature.

COUNT DOWN

Prepare and Freeze in Advance: Spicy Drumettes, Madeira-Glazed Turkey Breast, Spicy Flank Steak, and the Cider Vinegar-Glazed Ham.

TWO DAYS PRIOR

Make Fresh Raspberry Cheesecake, Lemon Pound Cake, Kings Cake Cupcakes, and the corn and pepper salsa for the Spicy Flank Steak. Keep refrigerated.

DAY PRIOR

Remove the Spicy Drumettes, Madeira-Glazed Turkey Breast, Spicy Flank Steak, and Cider Vinegar-Glazed Ham from the freezer and thaw. Make the Southern Praline Yams, Rosemary Dijon Potatoes, Wild Rice Salad with Cranberries and Pear Gallette.

DAY OF

Make Shrimp-Stuffed Baby Bellas (do not refrigerate and serve room temperature), Crab and Asiago Cheese Dip (keep refrigerated until the guests arrive), Grilled Asparagus Spears, Grilled Salmon (keep refrigerated until guests arrive), and Pear Gallette. Prepare Vegetable Platter, wrap in plastic and chill until guests arrive. Slice turkey, flank steak, and ham and arrange on separate platters. Fill baskets with crackers and French bread slices to serve with the Cranberry and Brie Canapés and Crab and Asiago Cheese Dip.

APPETIZERS

The Spicy Drumettes can be made in advance and frozen. Thaw the day prior to the open house and keep chilled until the guests arrive. The vegetables can be cleaned and prepared the day before and refrigerated. The day of the party, prepare the Vegetable Platter; wrap in plastic and chill until guests arrive. The Shrimp-Stuffed Baby Bellas should be made the day of the party and served at room temperature. The Crab and Asiago Cheese Dip should be made the day of the party and kept refrigerated until the guests arrive. Stilton Cheese Appetizer and Cranberry and Brie Canapés should be prepared the day of the party.

SALADS AND SIDE DISHES

The Southern Praline Yams, Rosemary Dijon Potatoes, and Wild Rice Salad with Cranberries can be made the day prior and kept refrigerated until the guests arrive. Grilled Asparagus Spears should be grilled the day of the party and kept refrigerated until the guests arrive.

MAIN DISHES

All of the main dishes, excluding the salmon (turkey, ham, and flank steak) can be made in advance and frozen. The day prior to the open house, remove from freezer and thaw. The day of the open house, slice all meats and arrange on separate platters. Keep platters chilled until the guests arrive. Salmon should be made the day of the party and kept refrigerated until the guests arrive. The corn and pepper salsa for the Spicy Flank Steak can be made 2 days ahead and kept refrigerated.

DESSERTS

The Fresh Raspberry Cheesecake, Lemon Pound Cake, and King Cake Cupcakes can be made 2 days ahead and kept refrigerated. Pear Gallette can be made the day prior and kept refrigerated.

Spicy Drumettes

Spicy Chicken Rub
1/4 cup packed brown sugar
1/4 cup sweet paprika
1/4 cup coarse salt
3 tablespoons cracked black pepper
1 tablespoon garlic powder
2 teaspoons celery seeds
1 teaspoon cayenne pepper

Cajun Rub
2 tablespoons coarse salt
2 tablespoons sweet paprika
1/2 tablespoon pressed garlic
1/2 tablespoon finely minced onion
1/2 tablespoon dried thyme leaves
1/2 tablespoon dried oregano
1/2 teaspoon ground bay leaf
1/2 tablespoon cracked black pepper
1/2 tablespoon cayenne pepper

Drumettes
5 pounds chicken drumettes

To prepare the spicy chicken rub, combine the brown sugar, paprika, salt, black pepper, garlic powder, celery seeds and cayenne pepper in a bowl and mix well to incorporate the seasonings into the brown sugar.

To prepare the Cajun rub, combine the salt, paprika, garlic, onion, thyme, oregano, bay leaf, black pepper and cayenne pepper in a bowl and mix well.

To prepare the drumettes, preheat the oven to 425 degrees. Mix the spicy chicken rub and Cajun rub together. Rub the mixture over the drumettes to coat well. Place in a lightly greased baking pan. Bake for 30 to 40 minutes or until the drumettes are cooked through and crispy.

Shrimp-Stuffed Baby Bellas

24 small baby bella mushrooms
12 uncooked small to medium shrimp, chopped
1 cup ricotta cheese
2 eggs
$1\frac{1}{2}$ cups Italian bread crumbs
$1\frac{1}{2}$ cups (6 ounces) grated Gruyère cheese

Preheat the oven to 400 degrees. Place each mushroom on a cutting surface and with a small paring knife remove the stems by cutting around the stem in a diagonal circular motion, being careful not to cut through the mushroom. (The stems should come out very easily and have a nice cavity for stuffing.) Discard the stems. Place the mushrooms cavity side up in a 9×13-inch baking dish.

Combine the shrimp, ricotta cheese, eggs, bread crumbs and Gruyère cheese in a medium bowl and mix well. Stuff 2 heaping tablespoons of the shrimp mixture into each mushroom, pushing the stuffing down into the mushroom and piling above the mushroom edge into a mound, using your fingers if necessary. Bake, uncovered, for 15 to 20 minutes or until the shrimp turn pink. Do not overbake. (The mushrooms should have a nice crunchy coating with a soft interior.)

Lisa Jensen

Stilton Cheese Appetizer

1 (2-pound) block of Stilton cheese
3 tablespoons port
Dried apricots
Water crackers

Place the cheese on a serving platter and pour the wine over the cheese. Let stand for 20 minutes to allow the wine to soak into the cheese. Serve with the apricots in a separate serving bowl. Provide a good cheese knife so that guests can slice the cheese and place on the crackers.

Cranberry and Brie Canapés

1 (8-ounce) round Brie cheese
1 tablespoon coarsely chopped cashews
1/4 cup whole cranberry sauce
Water crackers

Preheat the oven to 350 degrees. Lightly coat an ovenproof serving plate with vegetable oil. Place the cheese with the rind on in the center of the prepared plate. Bake, uncovered, for 8 to 10 minutes or until the cheese is partially melted. Top the cheese with the cashews and cranberry sauce. Serve immediately with water crackers.

Crab and Asiago Cheese Dip

1 cup sliced button mushrooms
1 teaspoon olive oil
1 cup coarsely chopped cooked lump crab meat (Buy a couple of precooked king crab legs, remove the crab meat from the shell and coarsely chop.)
1 cup mayonnaise (You may use light; but do not use fat-free.)
1 cup sour cream (You may use light; but do not use fat-free.)
3/4 cup (3 ounces) grated asiago cheese
1/2 cup sliced green onions

Preheat the oven to 350 degrees. Sauté the mushrooms in the olive oil in a small skillet over medium-high heat for 6 minutes. Mix the sautéed mushrooms, crab meat, mayonnaise, sour cream, cheese and green onions in a medium bowl. Spoon into a small baking dish sprayed with nonstick cooking spray. Bake, uncovered, for 35 minutes or until bubbly and the top is light golden brown.

Lisa Jensen

Grilled Asparagus Spears

$1^1/_2$ to 2 pounds fresh asparagus
Olive oil (optional)
Salt and pepper to taste
Sliced fresh red bell pepper rings

Preheat the grill to medium-high heat. Rinse the asparagus and cut off the tough ends. Brush lightly with olive oil. Lay the asparagus a few batches at a time crosswise on the grill rack. Grill for 3 to 5 minutes for thin spears, or 5 to 10 minutes for thicker spears, or until tender but still firm. Remove from the grill rack and season with salt and pepper. (You may toss the spears lightly with a vinegar- and oil-type dressing at this point.) Chill until ready to serve. Garnish with bell pepper rings just before serving. (The asparagus may also be steamed or stir-fried.)

Southern Praline Yams

3 cups mashed cooked yams
1/2 cup (1 stick) butter, melted
1/2 cup granulated sugar
2 eggs, well beaten
1 teaspoon vanilla extract
1/3 cup milk
1/2 cup whipping cream
1 cup packed light brown sugar
1/3 cup granulated sugar
1 cup pecans

Preheat the oven to 350 degrees. Combine the yams, butter, 1/2 cup granulated sugar, the eggs, vanilla and milk in a bowl and mix well. Spoon into a baking dish with tall sides to allow the topping to expand. (There should be at least 1 1/2 inches above the yam mixture.) Bake for 40 minutes. Remove from the oven and maintain the oven temperature.

Combine the cream, brown sugar, 1/3 cup granulated sugar and the pecans in a heavy saucepan and bring to a boil. Cook to 234 to 240 degrees on a candy thermometer, soft-ball stage. (The mixture will form a ball when a few drops of the mixture are dropped into cold water.) Spoon over the baked yam mixture. Return to the oven and bake for 10 minutes.

Rosemary Dijon Potatoes

1 1/2 pounds new potatoes
1 teaspoon salt
2 tablespoons olive oil
2 tablespoons minced shallots
2 tablespoons Dijon mustard
(Use the whole seed type for more texture.)
1 tablespoon chopped fresh rosemary
1/4 cup (1 ounce) grated Parmesan cheese
Salt to taste

Scrub the potatoes and leave the skin on. Cut the potatoes into halves and place in a large saucepan. Cover with water and add 1 teaspoon salt. Cook over medium-high heat for 15 minutes or until the potatoes are tender but still firm. Drain the potatoes and set aside.

Mix the olive oil, shallots, Dijon mustard and rosemary in a small saucepan. Cook over medium heat for 8 minutes. Add the mustard mixture and Parmesan cheese to the potatoes and toss until well coated. Season with salt to taste. Serve hot or chilled.

Wild Rice Salad with Cranberries

Partridgeberry Vinaigrette

1/4 cup partridgeberry vinegar or raspberry vinegar
(*See* Sources, pages 114–115.)
2 tablespoons olive oil
1 tablespoon soy sauce

Salad

1 package long grain and wild rice
(Uncle Ben's original recipe was used for testing.)
2 cups frozen corn, thawed
1/2 red onion, thinly sliced
1 cup chopped celery
3/4 cup chopped carrots
3/4 cup dried cranberries

To prepare the vinaigrette, whisk the vinegar, olive oil and soy sauce in a small bowl until blended.

To prepare the salad, cook the rice using the package directions. Add the corn, onion, celery, carrots and cranberries and mix well. Add the vinaigrette and toss to coat. Spoon into a serving bowl. (The salad can be made one day in advance and refrigerated.)

Lisa Jensen

Madeira-Glazed Turkey Breast

Madeira Glaze
2 tablespoons madeira
2 tablespoons dark molasses
2 tablespoons soy sauce
2 tablespoons red wine

Turkey
1 tablespoon olive oil
1 (5-pound) bone-in turkey breast
1 teaspoon dried thyme
1 teaspoon dried rosemary
1 teaspoon salt
1 teaspoon pepper

To prepare the glaze, combine the madeira, molasses, soy sauce and red wine in a small bowl and mix well.

To prepare the turkey, preheat the oven to 400 degrees. Brush the olive oil over the turkey. Rub the turkey with the thyme, rosemary, salt and pepper. Place the turkey in a roasting pan. Roast on the center oven rack for 15 minutes and then baste with the glaze. Continue to roast until a meat thermometer registers 180 degrees, basting every 10 minutes with the glaze. (You may also grill the turkey with excellent results.)

Lisa Jensen

Spicy Flank Steak with Corn and Pepper Salsa

Corn and Pepper Salsa

2 cups fresh corn kernels
3/4 cup chopped red and green bell peppers
1/2 cup chopped tomato
1/4 cup finely chopped red onion
1/2 tablespoon minced jalapeño chile
2 tablespoons chopped fresh cilantro
1 tablespoon olive oil
1 tablespoon fresh lemon juice or lime juice
1 teaspoon white wine vinegar
1/2 teaspoon salt
1/2 teaspoon pepper

Steak

1 (2-pound) flank steak
4 chipotle chiles in adobo sauce, chopped (The remaining chiles can be placed in a sealable freezer bag and frozen.)
1/2 cup of your favorite purchased salsa
2 tablespoons lemon juice or lime juice
1/4 cup balsamic vinegar

To prepare the corn and pepper salsa, mix the corn, bell peppers, tomato, onion, jalapeño chile and cilantro in a small bowl. Whisk the olive oil, lemon juice, wine vinegar, salt and pepper in a small bowl. Add to the corn mixture and mix well. Cover and chill in the refrigerator. (You may make one day ahead up to this point.)

To prepare the steak, place the steak in a large sealable plastic bag. Add the chipotle chiles in adobe sauce, salsa, lemon juice and balsamic vinegar and seal the bag. Rotate the bag to cover the steak with the marinade. Marinate in the refrigerator for 8 to 12 hours.

Preheat the grill to medium-high. Drain the steak, discarding the marinade. Place the steak on a grill rack. Grill for 6 minutes per side for medium-rare. (If you do not have access to a grill, the steak can be broiled. Six minutes per side under the broiler should provide similar results, however, check for the desired doneness.) Serve with the corn and pepper salsa. (Chipotle chiles in adobo sauce can be purchased in the Hispanic section of most grocery stores.)

Grilled Salmon

1/4 cup white wine
3 tablespoons sherry
3 tablespoons capers
1 tablespoon Dijon mustard or
country Dijon mustard
2 tablespoons olive oil
2 tablespoons lemon juice
1 teaspoon fresh dill weed
1 (1- to 1 1/2-pound) Atlantic salmon
(skinless or with skin)

Whisk the wine, sherry, capers, Dijon mustard, olive oil, lemon juice and dill weed in a small bowl until blended. Pour into a 1-gallon sealable plastic bag. Add the salmon and rotate the bag to cover with the marinade. Marinate in the refrigerator for 2 hours or longer.

Preheat the grill. Drain the salmon, discarding the marinade. Place the salmon on a grill rack and grill for 6 minutes. Using two long spatulas, carefully flip the salmon and grill for 5 to 6 minutes longer or to the desired degree of doneness. (If the salmon has the skin on it, grill skin side down first. When turning, the skin will easily come off after it has cooked on the one side.) Using two long spatulas, place on a fish platter. Garnish with sprigs of fresh parsley and lemon slices.

Lisa Jensen

Cider Vinegar-Glazed Ham

1 (7- to 8-pound) boneless precooked ham
1 small onion, minced
1 tablespoon butter
1 cup maple syrup
1/2 cup cider vinegar
1 tablespoon spicy mustard
1/2 teaspoon pepper

Preheat the oven to 350 degrees. Cut small sideways slits in the top of the ham. Sauté the onion in the butter in a medium sauté pan for 10 minutes or until soft and brown. Add the maple syrup, vinegar, spicy mustard and pepper. Cook over low heat until blended, stirring constantly. Place the ham in a baking dish. Pour the glaze over the ham. Roast, uncovered, for 1 hour, spooning the glaze over the ham every 15 minutes.

Lisa Jensen

Pear Galette

1 refrigerator pie pastry
3 tablespoons plus 1 teaspoon turbinado sugar
(Sugar in the Raw was used for testing.)
1 tablespoon lemon juice
1 to $1^1/_2$ Anjou pears, cored but not peeled
2 tablespoons butter, melted
$^1/_2$ teaspoon almond extract
Sliced almonds (optional)
2 to 3 tablespoons semi-soft sharp cheese,
such as asiago, Havarti or Gouda

Preheat the oven to 350 degrees. Roll the pastry into a 12-inch circle on a baking sheet lined with baking parchment. Sprinkle with 1 tablespoon of the sugar. Mix the lemon juice in a large bowl filled with chilled water. Cut the pears into very thin wedges and drop in the lemon water, making sure each wedge gets completely immersed. (This process keeps the pears from turning brown.) Remove the pear wedges from the water to paper towels to drain.

Arrange the pears in a decorative pattern on the pastry, leaving about 2 inches of space around the edge. Mix the butter and almond extract in a small bowl and brush over the pears. Sprinkle with 2 tablespoons of the sugar. Gather the 2-inch edge of the pastry over the fruit. Scatter the almonds over the top. Sprinkle with the cheese and the remaining 1 teaspoon sugar. Bake for 30 minutes. Remove from the oven and let cool for 5 minutes. Serve with ice cream or a dessert wine.

Jacqulin Rognehaugh and Donna Downey

Fresh Raspberry Cheesecake

Cinnamon Walnut Graham Cracker Crust

1 3/4 cups graham cracker crumbs
1 teaspoon ground cinnamon
1/4 cup walnuts, finely chopped
1/2 cup (1 stick) butter, melted

Cheesecake

3 eggs
1 cup sugar
1/4 teaspoon salt
16 ounces cream cheese, softened
2 teaspoons vanilla extract
1/2 teaspoon almond extract
3 cups sour cream
2 (6-ounce) baskets of raspberries, rinsed
Graham cracker crumbs for sprinkling (optional)
1/3 cup seedless raspberry jam
1 (6-ounce) basket of raspberries, rinsed

To prepare the crust, preheat the oven to 375 degrees. Mix the graham cracker crumbs, cinnamon and walnuts in a small mixing bowl. Add the butter and mix well. Place in the bottom of a 9-inch springform pan. Using your fingers, press the mixture over the bottom and halfway up the side of the pan. (It is okay if it's not perfect!).

To prepare the cheesecake, beat the eggs and sugar in a mixing bowl for 1 minute. Add the salt, cream cheese, vanilla and almond extract. Beat for 2 minutes. (It is okay if the mixture is not completely smooth.) Fold in the sour cream in 1 cup increments with a mixing spoon until the mixture is fairly even and smooth. Gently stir in two 6-ounce baskets of raspberries. Pour into the prepared springform pan. Sprinkle with additional graham cracker crumbs, if desired. Bake for 40 minutes. (The cheesecake should begin to crack in the center, but will still jiggle in the center when the pan is moved.) Remove from the oven and cool for 30 minutes. Chill in the springform pan for 8 to 12 hours. (The cheesecake must be thoroughly chilled in order to set.)

Heat the jam in a small saucepan for 2 minutes or until melted. Stir in one 6-ounce basket of raspberries. Spoon over the top of the cheesecake.

To serve, slide a knife around the edge of the pan and release the side of the pan. Keep the cheesecake on the bottom piece of the springform pan and place on a large serving platter.

Lisa Jensen

Chocolate Peppermint Roll

3 eggs
1 cup sugar
1/4 cup water
1/4 teaspoon salt
3 tablespoons baking cocoa
1 teaspoon vanilla extract
1/2 tablespoon butter, melted
1 cup all-purpose flour
1 1/4 teaspoons baking powder
1 tablespoon sugar
1 cup heavy whipping cream
10 pieces of hard peppermint candy
Your favorite chocolate sauce

Preheat the oven to 350 degrees. Beat the eggs and 1 cup sugar in a mixing bowl for 2 minutes or until thick. Add the water, salt, baking cocoa, vanilla, butter, flour and baking powder and beat for 3 minutes or until incorporated. Place a large piece of waxed paper on a 12×15-inch baking sheet. (The paper should cover the baking sheet.) Spray the waxed paper with cooking spray. Spread the chocolate batter evenly into a rectangle on the waxed paper. Bake for 15 minutes.

Sprinkle 1 tablespoon sugar on a 12×15-inch piece of waxed paper. Invert the cake onto the sugar-coated paper. Peel off the waxed paper from the top. Using the sugared waxed paper to help you roll, roll up the cake from the short end, leaving the waxed paper in as you roll. (The waxed paper will be removed later. When the cake is rolled up, it should be about 4 inches high.) Cool for 20 minutes. (This process helps the cake to keep its shape.)

Place the peppermint candy between two sheets of waxed paper and crush using a mallet. Whip the whipping cream in a mixing bowl for 15 minutes or until soft peaks form. Fold in the crushed peppermint candy.

To assemble the cake, unroll the cake and spread with the peppermint cream leaving a 1/4-inch edge around the cake. Reroll the cake, this time leaving out the waxed paper. Chill in the refrigerator.

To serve, cut the cake into 2-inch slices and pour your favorite chocolate sauce over the top.

Edith Jensen

Lemon Pound Cake

Cake

1/3 cup vegetable oil
1/2 cup 2% milk
1 1/2 cups all-purpose flour
1 cup sugar
2 eggs
1 tablespoon fresh lemon juice
1 teaspoon salt
1 teaspoon baking powder
1/2 cup chopped walnuts

Lemon Glaze

1/2 cup sugar
2 tablespoons fresh lemon juice

To prepare the cake, preheat the oven to 350 degrees. Spray a 6×11-inch loaf pan with cooking spray and sprinkle with all-purpose flour. Beat the oil, milk, 1 1/2 cups flour, the sugar and eggs in a medium mixing bowl until smooth. Add the lemon juice, salt and baking powder and beat for 30 seconds. Stir in the walnuts. Pour into the prepared pan and bake for 1 hour. Remove from the oven and cool in the pan for 20 minutes.

To prepare the glaze, mix the sugar and lemon juice in a small bowl until syrupy. Pour over the warm cake. Let stand for 30 minutes or until the glaze hardens on the cake. Remove the cake from the pan and place on a decorative platter.

A Kings Cake is traditionally served on January 6, the traditional twelfth day of Christmas. It is a way of celebrating the journey of the Magi to find the baby Jesus. Three jelly beans are hidden in the cake and the three who find a jelly bean in their piece of cake are declared one of the kings and pass out any gifts that are given that day. Gold foil-covered chocolate coins are also traditionally given on this day.

Kings Cake Cupcakes

1 (2-layer) package favorite cake mix
3 jelly beans (any flavor)
Favorite cake frosting
Cake sprinkles and candies

Prepare the cake mix using the package directions for cupcakes. Insert one jelly bean into the batter of three of the cupcakes. Bake using the package directions. Remove from the oven and cool on a wire rack. Spread the cooled cupcakes with the frosting and decorate with the sprinkles and candies. (The cupcakes should be very colorful.)

The Gallery

Photos

First Day…

A Pear Salad with Goat Cheese and Partridgeberry Dressing
B Quail with Port Sauce
Wild Rice with Mushrooms and Slivered Almonds
Green Beans Parmesan
C Berries en Papillote

Second Day…

A Black Turtle Bean Chili
Hearty Turtle Bread
B Turr-Turr-ific Turtle Dove Candy

Third Day…

A Rock Cornish Game Hens with Hen-of-the-Woods Sauce
Maitake Mushroom Risotto
Sautéed Asparagus with Tomatoes
B Cinnamon Apple Crepes

Fourth Day…

A Black Bean Cakes with Chipotle Aïoli
B Tomato Salad with Black Olives and Feta Cheese
Black Pepper Steaks with Bourbon Sauce
C Colly Bird Cookies

Fifth Day…

A Golden Brew Onion Rings
Golden Ring Pulled Pork Sandwich
Thai Noodle Slaw
B Five-Ring Pineapple Upside Down Cake

Sixth Day…

A Six-Egg Frittata
B Gooseberry Fruit Tart

Seventh Day…

A Swan Dive Endive
B Swan Lake Tilapia
Vegetable Couscous
C Swan Cream Puffs

Eighth Day…

A Creamy Onion Dressing with Tossed Greens Salad
B Milkmaid Sandwich
Sweet Potato Fries
C Black Cow Milk Shake

Ninth Day…

A Alligator Stomp Artichoke
B Dancing Shrimp Creole
Maque Choux
C Pecan Pie

Tenth Day…

A Lords of London Broil
Duchess Potatoes
House of Lords Brussels Sprouts
B Chocolate Orange Royale Cake

Eleventh Day…

A Fresh Tomato Bisque
B Peter Piper Pickled Platter
Piping Hot Pork Pie (Tourtiere)
C Cranberry Compote

Twelfth Day…

A Madeira-Glazed Turkey Breast
Spicy Flank Steak with Corn and Pepper Salsa
Cider Vinegar-Glazed Ham
Grilled Salmon
B Crab and Asiago Cheese Dip
C Cranberry and Brie Canapés
D Rosemary Dijon Potatoes
E Grilled Asparagus Spears
F Wild Rice Salad with Cranberries
G Pear Gallette
H Fresh Raspberry Cheesecake
I Chocolate Peppermint Roll
J Shrimp-Stuffed Baby Bellas

First day...

C

Second day...

Third day...

Fourth day...

Fifth day...

Sixth day...

Seventh day...

Eighth day...

Ninth day...

Tenth day...

Eleventh day...

Twelfth day...

Appendix

Sources

FIRST DAY NOTES

To order the partridgeberry vinegar and other partridgeberry products:
The Dark Tickle Company
P.O. Box 191
Griquet, NL
Canada
AOK 2XO
Tel/Fax: (709) 623 2354
www.darktickle.com

You may substitute the partridgeberry vinegar with raspberry vinegar, which can be found in most grocery stores.

1. Partridge or quail may not be easy to find at your local grocer, and so here are a couple of Web sites to assist you in ordering either tiny bird. You will need to purchase and prepare two per person. You can order by phone or via the Internet. If ordering over the Internet, it is best to call them directly first, as availability can be seasonal.

Oakwood Game Farm (best for ordering partridge)
P.O. Box 274
Princeton, MN 55371
Phone: (800) 328-6647
www.oakwoodgamefarm.com
Go to "Fresh & Smoked Game Birds" to find your selection.

Hickman Creek Hatcheries (best for ordering quail)
116 Ralls Road
Dover, TN 37058
www.hickmancreekhatcheries.com
Click on "Online Catalog", then click on "Fresh Farm Raised Gourmet Quail."

2. You may substitute partridge or quail with poussin, another name for a young chicken that is a bit smaller than the more popular Rock Cornish game hen. Or, substitute with Rock Cornish game hens (however we feature Rock Cornish game hens on day three).

3. Spatchcocking or deboning (optional): Lay partridge or quail breast side down on a cutting board. Cut flesh along either side of the backbone, 1/4 inch from the bone, and remove it. Turn the bird over. Press thumbs along breastbone firm enough to break up the bone. Turn the bird over again. Use a small knife or your fingers to remove the breastbone and ribs. Be careful not to tear or cut through the flesh and skin. (For your diners' convenience you can also remove the wings at this time.)

SECOND DAY NOTES

Dried black turtle beans are a staple in Caribbean and Latin American cooking and are the basically the same as plain dried black beans. If you can't find dried black beans in your local grocery store, they can be ordered from the Web site below:

www.harvestspicebasket.com

THIRD DAY NOTES

Fresh maitake mushrooms may be difficult to find, and so we feature dried versions that can be ordered from the following Web site:

www.edenfoods.com

Go to "Shop : Browse" at the bottom of the page. Then go to "Japanese Traditional" and then click on "Mushrooms." An .88 ounce bag can be purchased for around $7.00.

You will need one bag for our Three French Hens menu.

The maitake mushrooms can be substituted with any other mushroom.

FOURTH DAY NOTES

Chipotle peppers in adobo sauce can be purchased in the Hispanic section of most grocery stores. If you use the peppers in adobo sauce, use one pepper, chop well, and freeze the remaining peppers. These peppers are used in a future recipe on the Twelfth Day.

About the Authors

Donna Downey, the artist for our cover, currently lives in Colorado with her husband Pat. Other creative works done by her include paintings on silk.

Lisa Jensen grew up in Omaha, Nebraska. Her father owned Kenny's Restaurant, which was one of the best steak houses in the state for many years. Lisa moved to Phoenix, Arizona, in the 1980s and currently owns a residential and commercial painting company, but has loved to cook and entertain her entire life. Her father talked her out of the restaurant business, but ever since she was in her teens, the one thing most often said about Lisa is "Man, she sure throws a great party."

Jacqulin Rognehaugh is a fine artist. She lives in Nashville, Tennessee, with her husband Richard. Jacqulin and Donna Downey offer wonderfully unique gifts for the Twelve Days of Christmas on their Web site www.FreeEsprit.com.

Index

Order Information

Free Esprits
6991 South Poplar Way
Centennial City, Colorado 80112
(615) 351-1916
FreeEsprit.com

Name

Address

City State Zip

Telephone E-mail

Your Order	Quantity	Total
the Partridge and the Pear at $19.95 per book		$
Colorado residents add sales tax at $1.37 per book		$
Shipping and handling at $5.00 for first book; $2.00 for each additional book		$
	Total	$

Please make check payable to Free Esprits.

Payment may also be made by MasterCard, VISA or PayPal
when ordering online at www.FreeEsprit.com.

Photocopies will be accepted.